LOSING INTENSITY

The Story of Liverpool's 2022/23 Season

Pre-Season & Summer Transfer Window 2022

The dust had barely settled on the 2021/22 season. A mere thirty-nine days separated Liverpool's clash against Real Madrid in the Champions League Final and the first day of pre-season. Within that relatively short span, there were UEFA Nations League matches, creating a feeling that football had hardly taken a break.

The struggle to find enthusiasm for the upcoming season was a common sentiment for me and fellow fans on social media and various fan media platforms. The short break between seasons left little time to recharge and regain the energy and motivation needed for another demanding campaign. It didn't help that Liverpool's previous season's ambitions of a quadruple faded away in the last two matches, leaving anyone associated with the club with dreams of what could have been.

The disappointment of narrowly missing the Premier League title on the final day of a gruelling season was a tough pill to swallow. There was a glimmer of hope and excitement when Aston Villa took a 2-0 lead against Manchester City at the Etihad Stadium, fueling the belief that fate was on Liverpool's side. It seemed like a fairy tale, with Liverpool legend Steven Gerrard, then Aston Villa manager, potentially playing a role in delivering the league title to his former club. Unfortunately, the script didn't unfold that way, as Manchester City mounted a remarkable comeback, scoring three goals to win the game and secure the title. It was a bitter end to the Premier League campaign, leaving Liverpool and supporters disappointed.

The disappointment continued in the UEFA Champions League Final one week later. The distressing events that unfolded in Paris left Liverpool fans deeply unsettled. Fans were subjected to appalling treatment by inept French authorities at the Stade de France, and to make matters worse, they were unjustly blamed by French politicians and UEFA officials who should have known better than publicly accusing Liverpool fans without any evidence. It became clear that UEFA was attempting to divert attention from their failure to ensure a safe final. The entire episode was a disgraceful display, and the focus on football paled in comparison to the well-being and safety of the fans. It is understandable why supporters felt a more extended break was necessary, although the players, unfortunately, did not have that luxury.

Liverpool wasted no time in conducting their transfer business for the upcoming season. The club announced the acquisition of Fábio Carvalho in May 2022, securing the talented young playmaker for their squad. Liverpool initially attempted to sign Carvalho in January 2022 and loan him back to Fulham for the rest of the season, but unfortunately, it did not come to fruition. However, they persevered and completed the signing, with Carvalho officially joining Liverpool on the 1st of July. This signing appeared to be a shrewd move, as Carvalho was expected to further develop under the guidance of Jürgen Klopp and his coaching staff. Carvalho's transfer came in at a relatively modest cost, reportedly starting at £5 million and potentially rising to £7.7 million with additional add-ons.

Liverpool bolstered their squad further by signing talented Scottish right-back Calvin Ramsay from Aberdeen. Despite interest from Leeds United, who could have offered a more immediate path to first-team football, Ramsey opted to join Liverpool in a deal worth £4.2 million, with a potential additional £2.5 million in add-ons. At just eighteen years old, Ramsay was widely regarded as one of Scotland's most promising young players in his position. With a similar attacking mindset to Trent Alexander-Arnold, Ramsay's arrival *should* have provided valuable depth without compromising Liverpool's attacking style. Regrettably, Ramsey's playing time was severely restricted during his first season at Liverpool as he was sidelined with injuries for almost the entire campaign. Under the guidance of Klopp and his coaching staff, Ramsay can *still* develop his skills and hopefully fulfil his potential. Hopefully, he has put those injuries behind him now.

The high-profile signing of Darwin Núñez generated significant attention and excitement. The Uruguayan striker joined Liverpool from Benfica in a deal worth £64 million, which could rise to £85 million with achievable add-on bonuses. Núñez had already made a strong impression on Klopp and Liverpool during their quarter-final clash in the UEFA Champions League the previous season. He showcased his talent by scoring in both legs of the encounter. Klopp praised Núñez as an "extremely good-looking boy" and acknowledged his abilities as a solid player. Liverpool and Klopp are eager to see Núñez fulfil his potential and carve out a successful career at the club. Núñez scored fifteen goals and provided four assists in his first season, showing promise and making a valuable contribution to the team. While there is always room for improvement, his performance in his debut season was admirable.

Following the arrival of these three signings, Jürgen Klopp declared that Liverpool had concluded their transfer business. He expressed his contentment with the existing squad and stated that further transfers would only be considered if a player wanted to leave. To the surprise of many, Klopp later reversed his stance and acknowledged the need for another midfield signing. This change of heart resulted from recognising the potential impact early-season injuries could have on the whole campaign.

On transfer deadline day, Liverpool made a surprising move to secure the loan signing of Arthur Melo from Juventus. The Brazilian midfielder was not rumoured to be on Liverpool's radar, leading to surprise among fans and journalists upon his arrival. As part of the loan deal, Liverpool could purchase Arthur for a fee of £32 million in the summer of 2023 if they wanted to make the transfer permanent. However, Liverpool decided not to sign Arthur permanently after he only played thirteen minutes in the entire campaign. Arthur's signing was marred by a severe thigh injury that sidelined him for several months.

Unfortunately, his last-minute addition did not provide Klopp with the midfield depth he had hoped for, as the injury limited his playing time. The signing of Arthur may be seen as one of the worst signings of the Klopp era, highlighting the misjudgment in choosing a cheaper option over a more suitable midfielder. Being cost-effective is not always the best option.

Sadio Mané's departure from Liverpool to join Bayern Munich for £27.4 million generated mixed reactions among fans. Mané was seeking a fresh football challenge, and having achieved remarkable success with Liverpool; it seemed like the right time for a new chapter. However, his time in Germany did not pan out as expected, and he is anticipated to leave Bayern Munich in the summer of 2023. Mané's exceptional talent, remarkable work ethic, and invaluable contributions endeared him to Liverpool supporters, cementing his status as a true legend of the club. It was disappointing to witness his struggles in Munich, likely due to a physically demanding season with Liverpool. Nonetheless, his legacy at Liverpool remains intact, and his departure was undoubtedly a sad moment for the fans.

Divock Origi's departure from Liverpool to join AC Milan on a free transfer also marks the end of an era. Origi will be fondly remembered for his memorable goals and clutch performances at Liverpool. His ability to rise to the occasion and deliver crucial goals when the team needed them most had endeared him to the supporters. Recognising that his opportunities for regular playing time at Liverpool would be limited, Origi decided to join AC Milan, a move that was understood and respected by the fans. As he embarked on a new chapter in his career, Origi left on good terms, carrying with him the good wishes and gratitude of the Liverpool fans. Origi is another player who could have been more appreciated at his new club. During a match against Empoli in April 2023, Origi left the field to a chorus of boos and jeers from sections of the San Siro crowd, which wasn't nice to see.

Liverpool allowed more departures during the transfer window. Welsh defender Neco Williams secured a move to Nottingham Forest, offering him an opportunity with the newly promoted side. Takumi Minamino, who played a significant role in Liverpool's Carabao Cup and FA Cup campaigns, joined AS Monaco, departing with the best wishes of the club and supporters. Marko Grujić, after a loan spell at FC Porto, made a permanent move to the Portuguese club. Despite not appearing for Liverpool, Ben Davies found a new home at Rangers in Scotland. Sheyi Ojo, Ben Woodburn, and

Loris Karius left the club on free transfers. Ojo joined Cardiff, Woodburn headed to Preston, and Karius eventually found his way to Newcastle to cover for goalkeeper injuries. Sepp van den Berg and Rhys Williams embarked on loan spells, with Van den Berg joining Schalke and Williams joining Blackpool to gain valuable experience. Both teams were relegated, Blackpool from the EFL Championship and Schalke from the Bundesliga, which might have provided both players with some valuable experience.

Liverpool's pre-season training commenced on July 4th, marking the beginning of a new chapter. However, due to international commitments during the supposed summer break, some players had a delayed return to training. Liverpool understood the importance of rest and granted the players involved in UEFA Nations League matches some additional time off. The only challenge was coordinating the staggered returns of the players. Upon their return, the coaching staff put the players through the demanding lactate test. This rigorous fitness test measures lactic acid levels while increasing distances, gradually eliminating participants as their readings reach excessive levels. In an impressive display of endurance, 36-year-old James Milner emerged as the last man standing, securing victory in the test for the seventh consecutive year. Milner's remarkable feat is a testament to his unwavering commitment to maintaining peak physical condition.

Due to the COVID-19 restrictions, the team's ability to travel to other continents for pre-season had been limited. In the past, the squad has enjoyed training camps in Austria. However, Liverpool was fortunate to arrange a mini pre-season tour in Asia this season before returning to Austria for further preparations. These inter-continental pre-season tours testify to the global reach and excellent fan base. During these pre-season tours, Liverpool is always greeted by thousands of enthusiastic fans eagerly awaiting the arrival of their football idols. The warm reception the whole team receives reflects the fans' deep connection with the club. It is a testament to Liverpool fans' passion and loyalty, regardless of geographical location.

Billy Hogan, Liverpool Football Club CEO, expressed his appreciation for the warm reception received during the pre-season tour and recognised the incredible bond between the club and its fans across the globe:

It was certainly a busy few days when we were in Thailand. Having not travelled the last two years due to the pandemic, having the opportunity to get back on to the pre-season tours is great. Everybody enjoyed the experience. The reception was incredibly warm and enthusiastic, and it was great just landing at the airport in Bangkok when there were thousands of fans waiting for us, along with those outside the hotel. At every event we go to, the supporters are there. The reception has always been tremendous whenever we come to Thailand, and this time was no different.

Liverpool had travelled to Thailand to participate in the Bangkok Century Cup against Manchester United on July 12th. Unfortunately, the game's outcome was not in Liverpool's favour, as they suffered a 4-0 defeat. However, it is essential to remember that these matches primarily serve as fitness exercises rather than competitive fixtures. Jürgen Klopp approached the game with a focus on player fitness, as he fielded three teams, each playing thirty minutes. In contrast, Manchester United's new manager, Erik ten Hag, took a more serious approach by fielding a stronger starting eleven and making fewer substitutions. Although it is never pleasant to lose to a rival, it is better to experience defeat during the pre-season. The primary objective of these matches is to prepare the players physically and tactically for the upcoming season rather than focusing on the result, as hard as that is for the fans in attendance.

After visiting Thailand, Liverpool travelled to Singapore for the next leg of their Asian tour. They faced Crystal Palace in the Standard Chartered Singapore Trophy and emerged victorious with a 2-0 win. Jordan Henderson and Mohamed Salah were the goal scorers. Following the game, there were criticisms aimed at new signing Darwin Núñez regarding his performance. In response, Núñez took to social media, tweeting a 'shhh' emoji and the word "resilience." Given the transfer fee, it was understandable that Núñez was already facing pressure and expectations. However, expecting a rapid adaptation and instant success from a player is unrealistic. While Núñez's response on social media may not have been the best approach, it is essential to remember that he is human and subject to the emotions that come with criticism. Ideally, Núñez should have let his performances on the pitch do the talking to silence his critics. He needed time, patience, and support to settle into the team and showcase his abilities, and to some extent, even more so for his second season at the club.

After the squad visited Singapore, Liverpool travelled to Europe to face RB Leipzig in Germany. The match ended with a decisive 5-0 victory for Liverpool, with Darwin Núñez stealing the show by scoring four goals in the second half. This performance was the perfect response from Núñez, showcasing his abilities and silencing his critics. As previously mentioned, solid performances, hard work, and scoring goals are the most effective way to keep the critics at bay. Mohamed Salah also scored an early goal in the first half of the match against Leipzig. The result and performances indicated Liverpool was progressing and moving in the right direction as they fine-tuned their preparations for the upcoming season.

After their successful outing in Germany, the Liverpool squad moved to Austria for the next phase of their pre-season preparations. They set up camp in Saalfelden, a serene and picturesque town in the Salzburg region, which Klopp has favoured for training camps. The scenic backdrop of the nearby mountains provided a peaceful setting for the team. However, their purpose in Austria was not just to enjoy the scenery. Liverpool faced RB Salzburg in a friendly match, which ended in a 1-0 defeat for Liverpool. Klopp acknowledged that there were valuable lessons to be learned from this loss. During these pre-season matches, teams can identify areas for improvement and fine-tune their tactics and strategies before the start of the competitive season. Despite the defeat, the training camp in Austria allowed the team to continue their hard work and build on their fitness and tactics.

The squad returned to their home base, the AXA training centre in Liverpool, to finalise their preparations for the upcoming Community Shield match against Manchester City and the start of the Premier League season one week later.

As the Community Shield match approached, the excitement and anticipation among the fans grew, putting last season's misery of missing out on a possible quadruple behind them. They were willing to get behind the team again for another intense season. Liverpool aimed to start their campaign positively, setting their sights on achieving success domestically and in the various competitions they would participate in throughout the season. At this point, we were unaware of what difficulties lay ahead.

Liverpool 3 - 1 Man City

FA Community Shield
Saturday, 30th July 2022
King Power Stadium

Opinions on the Community Shield have always been divided. Some fans view it as a mere exhibition match, while others see it as a valuable piece of silverware. The perception often shifts based on the outcome. The losing team tends to downplay the significance, considering it a part of their pre-season preparations. On the other hand, the victorious team will emphasise its importance as an early trophy, fueling their hunger for further success in the upcoming season.

Due to the Women's European Cup Final scheduled for the next day at Wembley, The FA moved the Community Shield to Leicester City's King Power Stadium. The highly anticipated match featured Premier League champions Manchester City and FA Cup winners Liverpool, two teams with a recent history of intense competition. It was widely expected that these two sides would once again be in contention for the Premier League title in the upcoming season, but as we know with the fullness of time, those predictions were wide of the mark.

Before the 2022 Community Shield, Liverpool manager Jürgen Klopp had yet to secure a victory in the competition. In previous years, Liverpool had experienced defeats on penalties against both Arsenal in 2020 and Manchester City in 2019. However, at his third attempt, Klopp emerged triumphant, securing the one English trophy that had eluded him until then.

In the twenty-first minute of the match, Trent Alexander-Arnold broke the deadlock for Liverpool. The play unfolded as Thiago delivered a well-placed pass, floating it towards Mohamed Salah on the right side of Manchester City's penalty area. With great vision, Salah laid the ball off perfectly for Trent, who executed a seamless shot without breaking his stride. As the ball left Trent's foot, it took a deflection off Nathan Aké, who attempted to head it away from Manchester City's goal. Despite Aké's intervention, the ball continued to curl away from goalkeeper Ederson, hitting the inside of the post before finding the back of the net, giving Liverpool the lead.

Liverpool managed to maintain their lead until the sixty-ninth minute of the match. Kevin De Bruyne played a lobbed pass to Phil Foden, who showed good skill to get a shot off. Foden's effort, however, went straight at Adrián, who started the match due to injuries to both Alisson and Kelleher. Adrián allowed the ball to hit him, hoping to secure possession by diving onto the loose ball. However, Foden quickly reacted and contested the loose ball, causing a scramble in front of the goal. Unfortunately for Liverpool, the ball fell favourably for Julián Álvarez, who was just a couple of yards out and managed to slot it into the net. Adrián might feel he could have done better in that situation. While it wouldn't be fair to compare Adrián with Alisson, who is widely regarded as one of the best goalkeepers in the world, it's worth noting that Alisson would likely have caught the initial shot, effectively stopping City's attack. Adrián's parry resulted in a goal for Manchester City, tying the score at 1-1.

Darwin Núñez, Liverpool's new signing, made a significant impact when he entered the field as a substitute. His presence added a different dimension to Liverpool's attack, and it was during his time on the pitch that he played a crucial role in winning a penalty for the team. Salah delivered a lofted ball towards Núñez at the back post, and as Núñez attempted a headed shot, the ball struck the outstretched arm of Rúben Dias. Núñez immediately appealed to the referee for a penalty, but the play continued. However, with the video assistant referee's (VAR) assistance, the on-field referee, Craig Pawson, was advised to review the incident on the pitchside screen. After examining the replay, Pawson awarded Liverpool a penalty. Salah stepped up to take the penalty, striking the ball low and hard to Ederson's left, and despite the goalkeeper diving in the correct direction, he couldn't stop the ball from finding the back of the net.

In injury time, Liverpool extended their lead to 3-1 to secure the victory. Salah once again delivered a well-placed ball towards the back post, where Andy Robertson headed it back across the goal. Darwin Núñez, displaying quick thinking and athleticism, executed a sideways diving header to generate the necessary power for his shot to beat Ederson. Núñez's goal prompted an ecstatic celebration as he sprinted toward the Liverpool fans, who joyfully chanted his name to recognise his impact on the match.

Liverpool's determination to secure victory in the Community Shield was evident as they sought to show that they had moved past the disappointments of the previous season. Fans thought it was an opportunity to reaffirm their readiness to compete at the highest level again. Truthfully, it was one of Liverpool's better performances of the season.

The fact that their opponents were Manchester City, a team they have had fierce battles with in recent years, provided an additional incentive to succeed. Additionally, the trophy had eluded Liverpool during Jürgen Klopp's tenure, further fueling their motivation to claim the silverware. These factors undoubtedly contributed to Liverpool's strong desire to emerge triumphant in the match.

After the match, Manchester City's decision not to collect their runner-up medals sparked discussions and divided opinions. Some City fans argued that it showcased the team's winning mentality and refusal to accept anything but victory. However, others, including myself, interpreted it as a sign that Manchester City struggled with accepting defeat, and their actions were seen as petulant and disrespectful. It is worth noting that Manchester City had previously celebrated the Community Shield as part of their "Four-midable" campaign when they won all available English trophies in the 2018/19 season. The contrast of dismissing the runner-up medals after a loss but including the trophy in their promotional activities during their successful campaign was fascinating but not something Liverpool was in a position to exploit.

The day following their Community Shield triumph, Liverpool played a friendly match against Strasbourg at Anfield. The game's outcome saw Liverpool losing, with a 3-0 scoreline. Jürgen Klopp opted to field a significantly weakened side, with only a handful of first-team players in the lineup. The purpose of arranging this match was to provide valuable playing time for those squad members with limited involvement in the Community Shield encounter, allowing squad players to continue their preparations for the upcoming season.

Irrespective of the friendly defeat, Liverpool were glad to have won the Community Shield and earned an early victory against Manchester City. It had the potential to ignite the team's hunger for further success and set the tone for a promising campaign. However, this prediction turned out to be wide of the mark.

August
2022

- Fulham (A) - 6th August - EPL - Page 26

- Crystal Palace (H) - 15th August - EPL - Page 33

- Man. United (A) - 22nd August - EPL - Page 41

- Bournemouth (H) - 27th August - EPL - Page 49

- Newcastle (H) - 31st August - EPL - Page 56

Fulham 2 - 2 Liverpool

Premier League
Saturday, 6th August 2022
Craven Cottage

Liverpool's starting eleven for this game was not unexpected, except for Ibrahima Konaté, who was absent due to a knee injury. This led to Joël Matip partnering with Virgil van Dijk in defence. Another decision that could have sparked a discussion was the inclusion of Roberto Firmino over new signing Darwin Núñez, although it was not entirely surprising given Firmino's experience.

Despite the positive momentum gained from their victory in the Community Shield against Manchester City, Liverpool's performance against Fulham was unexpectedly lacklustre. The team seemed unable to match Fulham's high intensity, disappointing the fans who anticipated a solid start to the season. The contrast in performance was striking and left Liverpool supporters surprised and disheartened.

Before the game, Fulham manager Marco Silva's comments about his team not being ready for the beginning of the Premier League season seemed like a strategic move to downplay their chances against Liverpool. Many viewed it as a mind game aimed at easing the pressure on his side, especially considering they were facing a strong opponent in Liverpool. However, Fulham's performance proved quite the opposite of what Silva had suggested. They displayed a level of readiness and dominance that surpassed expectations, outplaying Liverpool for long periods and asserting themselves as the superior team during the match.

Aleksandar Mitrović proved to be a tough challenge for Liverpool's defence. Having scored an impressive forty-three goals in forty-four appearances the previous season, contributing massively to Fulham winning the EFL Championship, he showcased his talent against Liverpool through strength and determination. In the thirty-second minute, Mitrović scored the opening goal. It was a well-executed play as Kenny Tete delivered an excellent cross, which Mitrović met at the back post with a towering header. Trent Alexander-Arnold was out-jumped, and at first glance, it seemed that Trent could have shown more desire to win the ball or at least make it more difficult for Mitrović to score. However, doing that would have been easier said than done. Mitrović had the advantage of a running start and scored with his exceptional aerial strength. As a result, Fulham went into halftime with a 1-0 lead.

It's remarkable that Fulham only had 28% possession during the first half, as it felt like they had a larger share of the ball. This is a testament to the fact that possession alone does not guarantee victory; what a team does with the ball matters most. Despite Liverpool's three first-half shots, their closest opportunity to score came when Luis Díaz hit the post. With none of those shots on target, it can only be described as a disappointing half for Liverpool. On the other hand, Fulham thoroughly deserved their lead through their pressing and harrying in the first forty-five minutes.

Fulham came close to making it 2-0 early in the second half when Neeskens Kebano unleashed a shot that struck the inside of the post. Fortunately for Liverpool, the ball rebounded to Virgil van Dijk, who managed to clear it out for a corner.

Liverpool's first goal came after the 51st-minute substitutions, with Thiago making way for Harvey Elliot and Firmino being replaced by Darwin Núñez. The breakthrough for Liverpool arrived when Matip played a superb ball, cutting through Fulham's forward and midfield lines, finding Milner, who deftly touched it to Harvey Elliott. Elliott swiftly delivered a through ball into the path of Mohamed Salah, who had plenty of space on the right wing. With composure, Salah passed the ball across the box to Núñez, who tucked the ball away with a side-backheel finish. The goal was aesthetically pleasing, and the build-up play showcased the trademark style of this Liverpool side. Although I might sound critical, it's worth mentioning that Núñez had attempted a similar move a few minutes earlier without success. Nevertheless, a goal is a goal, and it was good to see him open his Premier League account. Liverpool had successfully equalised.

Unfortunately for Liverpool, their equalising goal was short-lived. Matip's sloppy and wayward pass near the halfway line resulted in losing possession, leaving Liverpool vulnerable and lacking defensive numbers. Bobby Decordova-Reid capitalised on the situation, passing the ball to the dangerous Mitrović. Virgil van Dijk attempted to tackle by sticking his foot out and inadvertently bought down the Serbian striker inside the penalty area. The replays indicated minimal contact, but Virgil's outstretched leg convinced the referee to award a penalty. Mitrović confidently stepped up, struck the ball with power and precision, and scored despite Alisson diving in the right direction. The penalty gave Fulham a 2-1 advantage.

Liverpool swiftly responded and found another equaliser soon after. Trent Alexander-Arnold displayed his ball-playing ability by delivering a well-placed ball into the box from a deep position. Fulham defender Tim Ream attempted to clear the ball with a header but failed to make the desired contact, causing it to flick unexpectedly into the path of Darwin Núñez. Caught off balance by the sudden opportunity, Núñez struggled to get a shot away, resulting in a heavy touch. Luckily, the ball fell perfectly into the path of Salah, who calmly side-footed it into the net. Liverpool had equalised for the second time.

Liverpool, unfortunately, did not manage to take the lead at any point during the match. In the game's dying moments, Liverpool had a late opportunity to secure all three points when Jordan Henderson struck the bar with a curling effort from outside the box. It would have been a magnificent goal had it been a few inches lower. Ultimately, the match ended as a 2-2 draw, which was disappointing. If anything, Fulham might have felt more disappointed because if there was one team that deserved to emerge victorious, it was them.

During a post-match conversation with Sky Sports, Jamie Carragher expressed his firm opinion that the performance by Jürgen Klopp's team was one of the worst he has witnessed. As an ex-Liverpool player, his statement carries weight. Although I cannot recall another performance from memory that was as poor as this, Carragher's assessment highlights how badly Liverpool played. Despite salvaging a point, it was one of those games that felt like a defeat.

At this early stage of the season, the dropped points left supporters feeling like Liverpool had already lost ground in the title race. However, it soon became apparent that the title race was not Liverpool's concern. The problem is that Manchester City and Liverpool have established a high standard, where achieving over ninety-plus point totals has become a regular occurrence. In some seasons, surpassing the ninety-five-point mark is necessary to secure the Premier League title. As a result, any points dropped can create a sense of lost ground, given the relentless demands and expectations set by these two top-performing teams.

I came across something post-match that was ridiculous. It revolved around the assumption that Liverpool would aim for around ninety-five points over the thirty-eight-game season, which allows for a maximum of nineteen dropped points. The standards and expectations set by Liverpool Football Club are undeniably high, making any dropped points feel huge. With this draw resulting in two dropped points, Liverpool had already exceeded 10% of their allocated allowance of dropped points if they wanted to challenge for the league title. This shows the immense pressure of competing at the highest level in the Premier League in the modern era.

The start of the new Premier League season was far from ideal for Liverpool. Failing to secure a victory against a newly promoted side, which they were expected to beat, was undoubtedly disappointing. Liverpool needed to find their rhythm and rectify any issues to avoid dropping further points. Liverpool could not afford additional setbacks to be in contention at the top end of the Premier League come May. The nine-day wait until their next game felt like a long time.

Liverpool 1 - 1 Crystal Palace

Premier League
Monday, 15th August 2022
Anfield

Following the draw with Fulham, it became clear through various Liverpool fan media channels that there was a desire for a midweek match to address the previous game's shortcomings swiftly. The hope was for an opportunity to rectify the situation sooner rather than later. However, Liverpool's schedule meant they had a nine-day wait until their next match against Crystal Palace. Unfortunately, the game's outcome was another disappointing draw, adding to the fans' frustration and disappointment.

Due to a training ground injury to Roberto Firmino, Darwin Núñez was given his first start for Liverpool. In a surprising change, Nat Phillips was included in the starting eleven, partnering with Virgil van Dijk in central defence. Ibrahima Konaté and Joël Matip were unavailable due to injuries and were not part of the match-day squad. Although back from injury, Joe Gomez was deemed fit enough for a place on the bench but did not start the game.

The inclusion of Nat Phillips in the starting lineup stirred up some social media outrage, with posts criticising Liverpool's "mediocrity." It was worth remembering that Phillips was, at best, Liverpool's fifth-choice centre-back and was only playing due to the team's injury situation. Similarly, James Milner faced criticism on social media following his inclusion in the starting eleven. Some sections of the fan base, specifically those advocating for #FSGOUT, used these selections to emphasise that Liverpool's owners, Fenway Sports Group (FSG), should invest more in the transfer window to improve squad depth. The outrage wasn't necessary because Nat Phillips and James Milner started the match regardless of online opinion, with the latter donning the captain's armband in the absence of Jordan Henderson, who was named on the bench.

Liverpool made a solid start to the game, showing their desire and determination in the early stages. However, Crystal Palace arrived at Anfield with a clear game plan. Deploying five players in defence, their objective was to contain Liverpool's attacks and exploit opportunities on the counter-attack. Despite enjoying a fair share of possession, Liverpool encountered difficulties breaking down Palace's well-organised and compact defence. The visitors' defensive solidity proved effective in frustrating Liverpool.

Before the match, a concerning statistic emerged, indicating that Liverpool had conceded the first goal in their previous five Premier League matches. However, four of those occurred towards the end of the last season. It remained a worrying trend that needed to be addressed. Considering the Champions League final against Real Madrid and the second leg of the Champions League semi-final against Villarreal from the previous season, Liverpool had fallen behind in their last seven competitive games. Unfortunately, Crystal Palace extended that streak to eight matches by scoring the first goal.

Crystal Palace executed their game plan flawlessly, resulting in a well-worked goal. Eberechi Eze managed to evade Fabinho's approach to win the ball far too easily, which granted Eze too much time and space to deliver a precisely weighted through ball to Wilfried Zaha. Nat Phillips seemed unsure whether to maintain the defensive line alongside Virgil van Dijk to employ the offside trap or track the quicker Zaha. At the last moment, Phillips attempted to play Zaha offside but failed to do so successfully. Zaha remained onside, gaining a significant advantage with half of the pitch at his disposal. Despite Virgil's efforts, he couldn't recover in time to provide cover, allowing Zaha to finish superbly with a side-footed shot into the far bottom corner. This goal put Crystal Palace ahead 1-0, and the score remained unchanged until halftime.

The second half took an unfortunate turn when Liverpool's newcomer, Darwin Núñez, let himself and the team down with a stupid outburst. Crystal Palace defender Joachim Andersen appeared to be purposefully provoking Núñez, constantly engaging in minor physical altercations and attempts to agitate him. The situation escalated as both players exchanged the agitator role. A compilation video showcasing their collisions and moments throughout the match gained traction on social media after the game, highlighting the heated exchanges between the two players. In a moment of poor judgment, Darwin Núñez fell into the trap set by Andersen and received a red card. Núñez initiated a confrontation with Anderson by leading with his head, leaving the referee with no option but to dismiss him from the match. It was a clear-cut red card offence, and Núñez's loss of composure proved costly for Liverpool. Already trailing 1-0, the team was now left with ten men on the pitch.

Going down to ten men ignited a renewed determination within the Liverpool team. Neil Atkinson from The Anfield Wrap (TAW), a Liverpool fan media channel, expressed his belief that this shouldn't be how football works. Having a numerical disadvantage should make the game more challenging, but Liverpool appeared to thrive in this instance. The team's intensity heightened, and the atmosphere at Anfield became more vibrant, with the crowd showing increased passion, frustration, and defiance. Surprisingly, Liverpool looked more threatening and had a greater likelihood of scoring, despite being a player short.

Luis Díaz scored an excellent equaliser for Liverpool, showcasing his brilliance. Starting with the ball on the left wing, Díaz showed exceptional close control as he weaved past five Crystal Palace players, skillfully evading their attempts to tackle him. His dribble allowed him to move centrally, positioning himself twenty yards from the goal, where he unleashed an unstoppable shot that found the back of the net. Alan Smith, providing co-commentary for Sky Sports, perfectly captured the moment, stating, "Well, he has just pulled Liverpool back into this single-handedly." I couldn't agree more. Díaz's goal was a testament to his ability.

Following Liverpool's equaliser, Crystal Palace had a golden opportunity to snatch victory. Wilfried Zaha found himself in a favourable position to score after a cross left the Liverpool defenders stranded and mere spectators. Opting to use his right foot instead of his left, Zaha's shot struck the outside of the post, allowing Liverpool to breathe a sigh of relief. Despite both teams' attempts, neither side found the winning goal, resulting in a 1-1 draw.

During Klopp's post-match interview, he provided insights into Liverpool's challenging week leading up to the match.

The week was crazy. I've experienced a lot of weeks, but that was like we had a witch in the building. Honestly, every day somebody else pulled up [with injuries] for the craziest reasons.

Klopp's post-match comment about the "Witch in the building" refers to lousy luck affecting Liverpool's injury situation. While *some* may interpret it as bad luck, I have a different perspective. The high number of muscle injuries could be attributed to potential mismanagement from a sports science standpoint. Overworking the players through constant high-intensity training can lead to strain and an increased risk of injury, mainly if training errors or excessive physical activity occur. This perspective suggests that a more careful approach to training and workload management could have reduced the number of muscle injuries within the team. These theories grew when news of unrest in Liverpool's medical department became public knowledge later in the season.

The extensive injury list included nine first-team injuries and Núñez's suspension, which undoubtedly took a toll on Liverpool and left them depleted in several positions. The number of injuries early in the season was more than a coincidence. Klopp highlighted the demanding nature of the previous season, where Liverpool played every game possible, and the players were required to maintain their peak fitness levels. Additionally, the earlier start to the season due to the World Cup in Qatar could have contributed to the strain on the squad. The combination of all these factors played a role in the high number of injuries at this stage of the season.

On a post-match podcast for The Anfield Wrap, Paul Cope highlighted a different perspective on another Klopp statement about extending pre-season into the season. Cope argued that mentioning this intention may have sent the wrong message to the players, potentially setting the wrong mentality within the squad. He suggested that if players were still training intensely as they would during pre-season, it could have been contributing to the high number of muscle injuries. Cope believed that the players would benefit more from rest instead. This viewpoint emphasises the importance of managing training intensity and workload to prevent injuries and ensure the players' well-being.

Despite my attempts to remain rational and acknowledge Liverpool's extensive injury list, I couldn't help but feel disappointed with their first two results. The significance of every dropped point was magnified due to the high standards set by Liverpool and Manchester City. For Liverpool to challenge for the Premier League title, they must strive for near-perfection or hope for a subpar season from Manchester City. Therefore, dropping four points in the initial two games was far from ideal. Fans certainly didn't want to witness a wasted season that felt like it was over before it started. Liverpool could have alleviated these concerns by swiftly finding some momentum, but supporters had to suffer again in an upcoming match before finally building some momentum.

Manchester Utd. 2 - 1 Liverpool

Premier League
Monday 22nd August 2022
Old Trafford

Liverpool's performance was disappointing on multiple levels. They were outmatched in determination, strategic thinking, and execution. The lack of desire and urgency displayed was also concerning, reflecting the state of things tactically and mentally. It was disheartening to find myself questioning the abilities of a Jürgen Klopp-led team, but the reality was that improvements were needed because the standards fell short of the mark. Continuously suggesting Liverpool's poor performances were solely due to their extensive injury list had become repetitive and boring.

The concerns extended beyond poor performances and results; it was the noticeable lack of resilience and determination from the players that were genuinely worrying. Their passive performances and lack of preparation were evident, particularly when faced with opposition pressure. While injuries may have played a role, it was crucial to recognise that using them as a universal excuse for every below-par performance is simply a way to deflect responsibility. The eleven players on the pitch needed to step up and rise to the occasion, leaving the injured players as secondary thoughts once the match began.

It must be acknowledged that Manchester United deserved the victory in this match. It pains me to admit this and even writing it feels unforgivable. How is it possible that Manchester United showed more determination? Liverpool has always been renowned as a team that fights relentlessly until the final whistle—known for their swift, overpowering style of play and overwhelming opponents with their never-say-die attitude. Something was seriously amiss at the point of the season. The passion and desire that once defined Liverpool seemed to have disappeared and was a significant cause for concern.

In addition to these concerning performances, Liverpool conceded the first goal again, continuing a troubling pattern that emerged in their last nine competitive matches. This trend posed a significant challenge for Liverpool in each game, creating an uphill battle every time. It is essential that this pattern was addressed and rectified, but Klopp and his staff seemed unsure of how to tackle it effectively. Clean sheets are the foundation for winning football matches, and

Liverpool's inability to prevent conceding first indicated the lack of a solid defensive base needed to secure victories.

Given Manchester United's disappointing start to the season, it was natural to expect a response. Their fast and energetic start to the game displayed a hunger to succeed, which was the opposite of their lacklustre performance in the previous week's 4-0 defeat against Brentford.

In the early stages of this game, Anthony Elanga had a moment that should have served as a wake-up call for Liverpool. Manchester United regained possession near the halfway line when Scott McTominay intercepted a poorly executed pass from Andy Robertson. With one well-executed forward pass from McTominay, chaos ensued in Liverpool's defensive line. The through ball reached Bruno Fernandes, leaving Liverpool defenders scrambling to recover. To regain control, Joe Gomez moved in to tackle, forcing Fernandes to slide and win the ball to keep it away from Gomez. Fernandes' subsequent sliding pass landed perfectly in the path of Elanga, whose shot struck the post. This was a lucky escape for Liverpool, and they refused to use it as an opportunity to wake up.

Trent Alexander-Arnold often faces criticism regarding his defensive abilities. Unfortunately, the first goal scored by

Manchester United only strengthened the arguments of those who doubted his defensive ability. Elanga played an easy one-two pass with Christian Eriksen in the build-up to the goal, effortlessly manoeuvring around Trent as if he wasn't even there. Elanga then played a ground pass to Jadon Sancho, who cleverly evaded James Milner's committed slide tackle/block attempt by faking a shot. This fake shot eliminated Milner from the equation and caused Alisson to dive to his left, anticipating a shot. Sancho coolly slotted the ball into the opposite corner to make it 1-0.

During the celebrations, the camera shifted from the celebrating Manchester United players to James Milner engaging in a confrontation with Virgil van Dijk. A visibly angry Milner voiced his disappointment about what Virgil should have done differently. Specifically, Milner emphasised that Virgil should have closed down Sancho, but instead, Virgil stood on the six-yard line with his hands behind his back, failing to make an effort to close the space and make it more challenging for Sancho to score. Milner's criticism was credible. Virgil should have moved toward Sancho to block the shot from a dangerous area. Confrontations of this nature are uncommon within Liverpool's squad, as their team spirit is usually flawless. However, this incident revealed a different dynamic within the team, a side we don't get to see often.

The attacking momentum graph for this match illustrated Manchester United's strong start. It also highlighted the periods when Liverpool had long spells of possession without being able to score, which was another concern. Analysing the data on the graph from sofascore.com, it is clear that Liverpool carried their attacking momentum from the first half into the beginning of the second half. However, unexpectedly, Manchester United managed to secure a second goal seemingly out of nowhere.

United's second goal came from nothing. Trent played a long ball into the United box, which Raphaël Varane headed away. The header came down for Jordan Henderson, who had plenty of space. However, Henderson's touch to control the ball was woeful, causing it to rebound off him and land directly into the path of Anthony Martial. Virgil attempted to challenge Martial, but Martial evaded the tackle and kept possession. At the halfway line, Henderson had an opportunity to make a professional foul against Martial, albeit resulting in a yellow card, but more importantly, halting United's dangerous attack. However, Henderson chose not to take this course of action, and Martial played a through ball to

Rashford, who found himself one-on-one with Alisson and scored. Irrespective of the circumstances, being 2-0 down at Old Trafford will always be tough to overturn.

Liverpool continued to attack to try and mount a comeback, but their efforts fell short. Meanwhile, Manchester United created promising scoring opportunities. Alisson had to make a crucial save in a crowded penalty area after a Marcus Rashford shot, which he struggled to see. Rashford had another effort, clearly full of confidence from his earlier goal. He embarked on a remarkable run, breezing past Trent as if invisible. He then deftly dribbled past an advancing Harvey Elliott before effortlessly gliding past Joe Gomez, who put minimal effort when attempting to tackle Rashford. Rashford got in a shooting position near the penalty area and narrowly missed the target with his shot, skimming it just above the crossbar.

When Liverpool finally managed to score, it happened from a corner kick. Trent delivered the ball into the box, but it was comfortably headed away by Diogo Dalot, who faced no challenge for the ball. The ball then found its way to Harvey Elliott just outside the box, and he headed it back into a dangerous area. Fábio Carvalho showed good control as he received the ball, quickly adjusting his body position, and executed a half-volley shot that forced David de Gea to make a save. The Manchester United goalkeeper reacted quickly, getting down low and producing a solid save requiring a firm hand. However, the ball deflected off De Gea's glove, and Mohamed Salah, showing great instinct, headed it into the net. Despite pulling a goal back, Liverpool failed to find another, meaning the game ended with a 2-1 victory for Manchester United, which only extended Liverpool's disappointing start to the season.

During this part of the season, I read Pepijn Lijnders' book, "Intensity." Despite Liverpool's struggles, I was determined to persist in reading it. One striking statement in the book resonated: "Intensity is our identity." This begged the question: Where had that intensity gone? Liverpool failed to demonstrate significant intensity in their first three Premier League matches. The team lacked fighting spirit and desire and had been notably off the pace. Every player in the squad fell under the umbrella of this criticism. There was an urgent need for improvement - a dire need for it to improve significantly. The level wasn't good enough.

It was challenging to identify the exact cause of the problem. Undoubtedly, Liverpool's numerous injuries have taken a toll, but why does it impact the players' performance on the field? Despite enjoying extended spells of possession, we struggled to convert that into goals. Liverpool's pattern of conceding the first goal added another difficulty to securing victories. Fans wondered if the players' hunger had diminished or if they had become burnt out. With many players having already achieved success and won numerous trophies, it was natural for fans to question whether they still possessed the same determination to continue winning. The struggles seen in the first three games had left fans with unanswered questions, making it challenging to find explanations for why some players couldn't execute even the basics correctly.

Liverpool 9 - 0 Bournemouth

Premier League
Saturday, 27th August 2022
Anfield

Liverpool desperately needed a convincing victory following their disappointing start to the season. It was essential not only to secure a win but also to deliver a commanding performance. In a remarkable turn of events, Liverpool rose to the occasion and achieved precisely that, demolishing Bournemouth with an astonishing 9-0 scoreline.

In his pre-match press conference, Jürgen Klopp provided insights into a team meeting held at the AXA training centre during the build-up to this game. Klopp expressed the importance of sitting down with the team and openly discussing his thoughts, which left him feeling relieved. He emphasised that the purpose of the meeting was to express himself rather than shout or criticise the players. Whatever happened during the meeting undeniably sparked a significant reaction from the players.

When the referee blew the whistle, Liverpool showed remarkable readiness and determination. They immediately gained control of the game, showcasing a level of dominance and drive that was noticeably absent in their previous defeat against Manchester United just five days earlier. Thanks to their quick start, Liverpool established a commanding 2-0 lead within six minutes of play.

Liverpool opened the scoring with a superbly delivered cross from Roberto Firmino, met by a powerful header from Luis Díaz. The video assistant referee (VAR) conducted a thorough check for offside, but thankfully, Díaz was onside. Interestingly, Díaz played a more central role in this match, deviating from his usual position of hugging the left touchline. This tactical adjustment made him appear significantly more threatening when in possession. Liverpool's wingers had found themselves isolated by remaining out wide, resulting in less involvement in the game, so it was an intelligent tactical change.

Liverpool swiftly added a second goal within minutes of their opener. Mohamed Salah, positioned on the right wing, skillfully dribbled his way towards the penalty area. Meanwhile, Roberto Firmino gestured for the ball outside the box by extending his arms. Salah passed the ball to him, and as the ball rolled across Firmino's body, he deftly touched it with his left foot, setting it perfectly into the path of Harvey

Elliott. Elliott, positioned just outside the box, curled a low shot into the net. It remained uncertain whether Firmino's touch was an intentional moment of brilliance or a lucky heavy touch that found a player.

However, Firmino's subsequent gesture towards the ball after the contact may sway some to believe it was intentional. Regardless, Elliott capitalised on the shooting opportunity, displaying composure and skill to score a splendid goal. He is one of the only players who could have made a reasonable argument to escape the criticism for his performances during Liverpool's slow start to the season, so I was glad he had a moment to celebrate. An emotional Elliott cried during the celebrations for his goal. Like many others, I assumed it was because of his season-ruining injury the season prior. This release of emotion showed he was back after the rollercoaster he must have been on after physiotherapy, regaining fitness, and then getting back into the team. However, during an interview with LFCTV after the match, Elliott said his grandmother sadly passed away during the week, which explained his emotional reaction. Elliott dedicated his goal and Liverpool's three points to his grandmother.

Liverpool's hunger for more goals was evident even after taking a 2-0 lead within six minutes. They were determined to extend their lead further and make a resounding statement. The team achieved this with a spectacular third goal, courtesy of Trent Alexander-Arnold. Positioned centrally on the pitch, Trent initiated a one-two pass with Firmino, who again deftly laid the ball off. Seizing the opportunity, Trent took a touch before unleashing a powerful strike from approximately twenty yards out. The ball flew into the net with astonishing power, leaving the goalkeeper with virtually no chance of saving it. As Trent celebrated, he nonchalantly shrugged, seemingly saying, "What did you expect?"

Liverpool's fourth goal was a stroke of fortune. Mohamed Salah advanced towards the penalty area from the wing and encountered a congested Bournemouth defence. Recognising the circumstances, Salah opted to pass the ball back to Trent instead of attempting to navigate through the maze of defenders. However, luck intervened when Salah's pass inadvertently deflected off a Bournemouth player who instinctively extended his foot in an attempt to intercept the ball. The deflection caused the ball to float perfectly into the six-yard area, where a quick-thinking Roberto Firmino capitalised with a precise volley. Though undeniably fortunate, the goal extended their lead to a commanding 4-0.

Liverpool extended their lead even further with their fifth goal before halftime. Andy Robertson's corner kick was expertly delivered, finding its way into the box, where Virgil van Dijk rose above the defence and headed the ball into the net. Seeing Trent Alexander-Arnold and Virgil van Dijk contributing to the scoresheet was a welcome sight. In recent matches, both players faced criticism for their performances, particularly in the disappointing showing against Manchester United, and supporters hoped both players were getting back to their best.

Despite holding a commanding five-goal lead, Liverpool continued their relentless pursuit of victory by refusing to ease off in the second half. They approached the second half with the same determination as the first and wasted no time adding more goals to their tally. Just seconds after the restart, Trent delivered a dangerous ball into the box from a wide position. Aware of the looming threat of Luis Díaz, Bournemouth defender Chris Mepham attempted to intervene and prevent an easy tap-in goal. Unfortunately for Mepham, his contact with the ball resulted in an own goal, extending Liverpool's advantage even further. Liverpool's unwavering hunger for goals was a welcome sight, and they played relentlessly.

Liverpool's seventh goal came from a clever corner routine. Instead of opting for a direct delivery into the box, Andy Robertson chose to play a short pass to Fábio Carvalho, who awaited Robertson's overlapping run on the outside before returning the pass. Robertson then unleashed a menacing cross into the box, but unfortunately, no Liverpool player managed to connect with it. The cross, however, posed a significant challenge for Bournemouth goalkeeper Mark Travers, who had to make a late diving save to keep it out. Regrettably for Travers, his save fell perfectly to Roberto Firmino, who was in the right place at the right time to convert the tap-in and score Liverpool's seventh goal.

To add insult to injury, Liverpool struck again for their eighth goal. Trent showcased his excellent passing range by delivering a lofted cross-field pass to Kostas Tsimikas, who showed great composure to play a precise pass back to Fábio Carvalho. Carvalho hit a stunning volley that found the back of the net, sending the Anfield crowd into celebration once more.

The goal-scoring didn't end there. Liverpool, relentless in their pursuit of victory, managed to find the back of the net again, this time from another corner. Tsimikas stepped up to take the corner to deliver a pinpoint cross, and Luis Díaz rose above the Bournemouth defence, directing a powerful header into the goal. The scoreline now read a staggering 9-0 to Liverpool.

The Liverpool faithful were hungry for more, their chants reverberating around the stadium with requests for a tenth goal, their desire for attacking football still needed to be fulfilled. Even with a commanding 9-0 lead, the fans demanded that the team continue the onslaught.

Dismissing or downplaying the significance of this emphatic result by labelling the opposition as "only Bournemouth" is a hollow argument. Bournemouth is a Premier League team and deserves equal recognition and respect. Rather than diminishing the result's significance, we should commend Liverpool for their impressive display against a fellow Premier League side. Liverpool executed their game plan perfectly, showcasing their skill and determination, which had been absent in the matches before this one. Thankfully, there were a few more matches throughout the season with emphatic scorelines like this.

Liverpool 2 - 1 Newcastle

Premier League
Wednesday, 31st August 2022
Anfield

You can't win 9-0 every match. Occasionally, you require luck and a last-minute goal to secure the three points. Throughout this game, there were moments where it appeared that Liverpool might not come away with a victory. Newcastle's performance was strong, making it a challenging contest and showcasing their defensive resilience. Before the match, Jürgen Klopp acknowledged that Newcastle is the most improved team in the Premier League, and it is difficult to dispute that claim. They have elevated their game massively compared to the era under the previous owner, Mike Ashley.

Liverpool understandably fielded the same starting lineup that got the resounding 9-0 victory over Bournemouth four days prior. If such an emphatic win doesn't secure a player's spot for the next match, it's hard to imagine what would. However, Newcastle took the lead, continuing Liverpool's trend of conceding the first goal. Despite hopes that the clean sheet against Bournemouth had ended this pattern, Alisson had little chance of preventing the goal. While defending against Newcastle's attack that led to their goal, Liverpool had players positioned to cover the threat. However, Jordan Henderson's attempt to intercept a pass only resulted in a lucky roll of the ball, which fell kindly to Sean Longstaff. Fabinho reacted quickly to close down Longstaff, leaving Alexander Isak with too much space to exploit. Additionally, Virgil van Dijk was pulled out of position by Miguel Almirón's movement, preventing him from effectively snuffing out the danger or being in the right place to make a tackle. Longstaff managed to play a well-timed pass through to Isak, who unleashed a powerful first-time shot into the roof of the net.

Early in the second half, Isak appeared to have scored another goal, but it was disallowed for offside. With a few well-executed feints, Isak bypassed the defensive efforts of Andy Robertson and Joe Gomez before unleashing another powerful shot past an advancing Alisson. However, VAR intervened and confirmed that Isak had been marginally offside. Despite the disallowed goal, Isak displayed his danger and composure on the field, unfazed by Anfield or the crowd.

Newcastle employed various time-wasting tactics from the dark arts playbook to disrupt the game's flow. Whenever the ball went out of play, their players conveniently suffered from muscle cramps, exhaustion, or feigned injuries, further prolonging stoppages and wasting more time. These tactics can be incredibly frustrating, not only for the opposing team but also for the supporters witnessing it.

Liverpool's equalising goal showcased their ability to transition from defence to attack quickly. Alisson initiated the move by rolling the ball out to Fabinho, who wasted no time playing a penetrating pass through the lines to find Harvey Elliott. Elliott showed his vision and awareness and swiftly passed the ball to Salah. Salah controlled the ball and patiently waited for his teammates to enter the box. With perfect timing, Salah threaded a pass into the path of the advancing Roberto Firmino, who calmly dispatched a well-placed shot into the bottom corner, equalising with a clinical finish. The seamless coordination and execution of this swift attacking sequence resulted in a crucial goal for Liverpool.

The attacking momentum graph for this match illustrated Liverpool's domination in the second half. They showed control with possession and constantly tried to break through Newcastle's resolute defence. However, despite Liverpool's dominance, it took some time before Liverpool found the equalising goal.

After witnessing Newcastle's time-wasting tactics throughout the match, there was a sense of poetic justice when Fábio Carvalho scored the winning goal in the dying moments. The game extended into the ninety-eighth minute because of additional injury time granted by referee Andre Marriner. Although the fourth official had initially indicated five minutes of added time, Marriner rightfully added extra time to account for the continued time-wasting tactics employed by Newcastle, with Nick Pope being the latest player to feign injury as the seconds counted down.

The decisive goal came from a corner kick delivered by James Milner. Joe Gomez leapt to connect with a header, directing the ball towards the back post and causing a chaotic scramble in the box. Amidst the chaos, Mohamed Salah got a slight touch on the ball, sending it into the path of Fábio Carvalho. With quick instinct, Carvalho turned and unleashed a close-range volley that thundered against the underside of the crossbar before finding the back of the net, securing a dramatic 2-1 victory for Liverpool in the game's final moments.

Neil Atkinson from TAW made a great point post-match by suggesting that if Newcastle had approached the game differently, they could have posed even more significant problems for Liverpool without resorting to dark-art tactics. Neil continued that Newcastle had already demonstrated their attacking threat and could have potentially secured a comfortable victory if they had continued to press forward. However, their decision to employ time-wasting strategies, and defend deep to frustrate Liverpool, ultimately backfired, leading to their downfall in the match. I share this sentiment that Newcastle missed an opportunity to win the game.

Although Liverpool managed to secure the victory and collect the valuable three points, it was apparent that their performance still didn't meet their usual high standards. Certain players appeared to lack sharpness and displayed signs of sluggishness. While fortune may have played a role in winning the three points, it was not a sustainable strategy for Liverpool to rely solely on luck in every match. Nevertheless, it is essential to acknowledge that earning three points is always preferable to none, regardless of how they are gained.

September
2022

- Everton (A) - 3rd September - EPL - Page 64

- Napoli (A) - 7th September - UCL - Page 72

- Ajax (H) - 13th September - UCL - Page 80

Following the passing of Queen Elizabeth II, the Premier League postponed all EPL matches, meaning Liverpool's fixtures against Wolverhampton Wanderers on Saturday, September 10th, and Chelsea on Sunday, September 18th, were delayed. These postponements were made out of respect and to allow for a mourning period.

Everton 0 - 0 Liverpool

Premier League
Saturday, 3rd September 2022
Goodison Park

Jürgen Klopp's post-match comment about the importance of *not* losing the derby held some truth. A loss can feel devastating in a high-stakes match like the Merseyside derby. While a draw wasn't the ideal outcome, it was seen as a fair result considering neither team did enough to win, and both goalkeepers had good games, making important saves and keeping their teams in the match. Avoiding defeat prevented further negative impacts on morale.

Liverpool's poor performances had left fans and journalists questioning what might be amiss. According to Phil McNulty of the BBC, the key players for Liverpool were performing below their usual high standards. James Nalton from This Is Anfield (TIA) suggested that this could be the lingering effect from the previous season. It *does* feel reminiscent of a hangover from the last campaign, where the team endured the mental and physical strain of competing in all competitions and narrowly missing out on achieving a historic quadruple. Such an intense pursuit would leave a lasting impact on both the mind and body of the players.

The quote from the Rocky film franchise, "It's not how hard you can hit, it's how hard you can get hit and keep moving forward," carries a sense of irony, considering Sylvester Stallone's association with Everton. However, the Liverpool players may have been experiencing fatigue from repeatedly having to bounce back after falling short in recent seasons. This could have led to a negative mindset where they realise that even giving their utmost effort and maintaining a high level of performance throughout a whole season still does not guarantee success in the sport's biggest competitions.

Klopp made several changes to the starting eleven for this match, opting to rotate the squad. Kostas Tsimikas started at left back instead of Andy Robertson, while Darwin Núñez returned to the lineup after serving his suspension. Fábio Carvalho was also handed his first start in midfield. Tsimikas showcased his abilities by getting into good positions on the pitch, which allowed him to deliver several good crosses. He showed intelligence and aggression without being overwhelmed by the significance of the derby. Overall,

Tsimikas had an excellent performance and contributed positively to the team.

Núñez demonstrated moments of promise throughout the match, with a few opportunities that showcased his abilities. While he could have been more clinical in certain instances, one shot stood out as a glimpse of his potential. Núñez made a well-timed run behind the Everton defence, expertly controlling the ball with his chest to maintain his momentum, and struck a half-volley that forced a save from Everton goalkeeper Jordan Pickford. Following the save, Luis Díaz took possession of the loose ball and took a shot that unfortunately hit the post. These two chances represented the closest Liverpool came to finding the back of the net.

Carvalho seemed out of his comfort zone and lost in midfield. Unfortunately, he had to be substituted at halftime following a knee collision with Everton's Amadou Onana, which looked painful. It was clear that he needed some time to settle in. However, this particular opportunity did not work in his favour.

At halftime, Klopp made a tactical change by bringing in Roberto Firmino and transitioning to a more aggressive 4-2-4 formation. Firmino's introduction injected more of an attacking threat into Liverpool's gameplay, and in the early stages of the second half, it seemed like a goal for Liverpool was imminent. Firmino unleashed several shots brilliantly saved by Pickford, which, under different circumstances, would have found the back of the net.

Jordan Pickford proved to be a worthy player-of-the-match winner. He pulled off a total of eight saves, including some incredible fingertip saves at full stretch, and each one of them played a crucial role in Everton getting a point. His most impressive save arrived in the game's latter stages when he swiftly reacted to a near-post shot from Salah, using his fingertips to redirect the ball onto the post. It was pivotal for Liverpool to clinch all three points, but Pickford's save denied them. As the match progressed, and with each save, Pickford's confidence seemed to soar.

Alisson also played a vital role in the match by making crucial saves. In the second half, he produced a superb stop from a shot by Neal Maupay, a chance that the Frenchman should have converted. Alisson also expertly adjusted his positioning when faced with a Dwight McNeil shot that deflected off Virgil. With impeccable footwork, he swiftly got into the correct position and showed lightning-fast reactions, managing to reach the ball with his fingertips and tip it over the crossbar.

Klopp made a double substitution in both fullback positions in the fifty-ninth minute. Andy Robertson replaced Kostas Tsimikas, while James Milner came on for Trent Alexander-Arnold. Surprisingly, these changes resulted in Liverpool having less control over the game. Anthony Gordon of Everton seemed particularly eager to take advantage of facing a thirty-six-year-old Milner, and Everton capitalised on Liverpool's temporary loss of control. Everton enjoyed their most dominant spell during this period, creating several scoring opportunities they should have converted. Fortunately for Liverpool, Alisson's exceptional goalkeeping prevented Everton from finding the back of the net.

However, there was a moment when Everton believed they had scored. Former Liverpool player Conor Coady found the back of the net at the back post and celebrated enthusiastically as if he had hit the jackpot. Thankfully, VAR intervened and confirmed that Coady was offside. Coady must have regretted his excessive celebration. The camera captured Núñez joking with Coady after the referee disallowed the goal. It appeared that Coady did not appreciate being laughed at.

After observing Everton's mini-revival, Klopp responded by making additional changes to counter their momentum. Joël

Matip was introduced as a centre-back, which enabled Joe Gomez to shift to the right-back position, and James Milner moved into midfield. Additionally, Diogo Jota made his way onto the field, replacing Núñez, but sadly, Liverpool couldn't find a winning goal.

While the draw against Everton was disappointing, I found solace in that draws are a common outcome in Merseyside derbies at Goodison Park. Out of the past eleven matches played there, ten have ended in draws, highlighting the challenging nature of the venue even during Liverpool's successful seasons. However, it was clear that Liverpool still needed to improve.

On a positive note, Alisson's impressive saves prevented Liverpool from experiencing an embarrassing defeat, and Virgil appeared to regain some form compared to recent weeks. These factors provided some encouraging aspects amidst the disappointment.

The post-match tweets by analyst Dan Kennett regarding Liverpool's running stats raised concerns. According to Dan, Liverpool had been outrun by their opponents in every game at this point in the season, with the opponent's total distance covered surpassing Liverpool's. Additionally, Dan noted that Liverpool had fewer high-intensity runs than their opponents in each game. This data indicated that Liverpool's players were being outworked and outpaced by their opponents, which is alarming considering Liverpool's reputation under Jürgen Klopp for their relentless work ethic and high-intensity style of play. Typically, Liverpool prides itself on going further and pushing harder than any team they face, which shows their strength as a team. The data suggest deviations from their expected performance levels, highlighting improvement areas.

Understandably, the squad struggled to maintain the high levels we were accustomed to, considering the physical toll of the previous season and the limited time for rest during the summer break. The combination of an exhausting campaign and a condensed pre-season undoubtedly took a toll on the players, leading to physical and mental fatigue. When the body is fatigued, it can significantly impact decision-making and overall performance, which might explain the players' subpar performances and poor decision-making. The demanding schedule and limited recovery time had likely contributed to these challenges, emphasising the importance of managing player fatigue and ensuring sufficient rest and recovery periods.

The points total for Liverpool at this stage of the season could have been better, with only nine out of a possible eighteen accumulated. The schedule was about to change to three games per week until the World Cup break in November, which presented a perfect time for Liverpool to develop a winning streak and find consistency. Unfortunately, things got worse before they got better.

Napoli 4 - 1 Liverpool

UEFA Champions League (Matchday 1)
Wednesday, 7th September 2022
Diego Armando Maradona Stadium

This performance was undoubtedly one of the most disappointing and frustrating that Liverpool fans had witnessed in a long time. While Liverpool already had its fair share of poor showings this season, this match was particularly disheartening. The team's performance in this game reached a new low and fell short of our expected standards.

Napoli wasted no time causing trouble for Liverpool, exploiting Liverpool's defensive line within seconds. A high ball played over Liverpool's backline bypassed the defence effortlessly. Victor Osimhen demonstrated perfect timing with his run, breaking through our high line and reaching the ball before an advancing Alisson. Osimhen attempted a shot from a difficult angle, only to see it strike outside the post, providing a lucky escape for Liverpool. Napoli created this first scoring opportunity within forty seconds, highlighting their immediate threat to Liverpool's defence.

Just three minutes later, Napoli *again* exploited Liverpool's high defensive line with a lobbed through ball. This time, Napoli showed patience, slowing down the play to allow more players to join the attack. Eventually, the ball reached Matteo Politano, whose shot appeared well blocked by James Milner. However, upon reviewing the replay, it became evident that the ball had struck Milner's outstretched hand, leaving the referee with no choice but to award a penalty. Piotr Zieliński stepped up to take the penalty and successfully converted it, putting Napoli ahead with a 1-0 lead.

Around the fifteen-minute mark, Liverpool encountered more difficulties with another well-placed ball. Once again, Osimhen was played through, but Virgil van Dijk closely marked him this time. A physical battle ensued as they both vied for possession while entering the penalty area. Although the contact appeared minimal, VAR advised the on-field referee to review the replay. Virgil unintentionally stepped on Osimhen's foot in the clash between the two players, resulting in the referee awarding another penalty. This decision may have seemed harsh, given the speed of the incident and the lack of intention. Osimhen stepped up to take the penalty, but

Alisson made a crucial save, denying him and keeping the score at 1-0.

Napoli had another clear scoring opportunity shortly after, which they should have capitalised on. Once again, their dangerous striker Osimhen was played through, but Joe Gomez tried to provide cover defensively. In hindsight, it would have been wiser for Gomez to clear the ball out of play, conceding a throw-in. This decision would have allowed Liverpool players to regroup and position themselves defensively. However, Gomez opted to take a touch, allowing Osimhen to regain possession by stealing the ball away from Gomez in a dangerous area. Osimhen, who displayed admirable unselfishness, passed the ball to Khvicha Kvaratskhelia, whose shot was cleared off the goal line by Virgil. Somehow, the scoreline remained 1-0, but this would not be the case for long.

Liverpool's performance in this match can be summed up by analysing the replay of Napoli's second goal. Once again, Joe Gomez found himself dispossessed, putting Liverpool in a vulnerable position. Napoli deliberately slowed down the play, allowing their teammates to join the attack, allowing Liverpool to regroup defensively. André-Frank Zambo Anguissa executed a simple one-two pass with Zieliński before calmly slotting the ball past Alisson to secure Napoli's second goal. Notably, Trent Alexander-Arnold, Harvey Elliott, and Fabinho were positioned near the inter-passing players during the one-two pass. However, no one tracked Anguissa after he played the pass, and there was a lack of effort and desire to mark him as he made his way into the box to receive the return pass. Furthermore, there was a notable absence of attempts to intercept the pass or showcase any defensive determination from every Liverpool player on the pitch. Napoli seemed to navigate through Liverpool's defence with ease, and the defending by Liverpool in this situation was undeniably unforgivable.

Liverpool's conceded yet another disappointing and embarrassingly easy goal. Kvaratskhelia effortlessly bypassed Trent with alarming ease, highlighting the Liverpool defence's current struggles. While it's important not to solely single out individual players, in hindsight, Trent could have benefited from some time on the bench to realise that his place in the starting eleven was not guaranteed and to take him out of the firing line. However, it remained hypothetical, as Trent kept his position in the team regardless of his performance level. As mentioned, Kvaratskhelia ran past Trent as if he wasn't there, progressing into the box where he encountered a physical battle with Gomez. Gomez was easily shrugged off, and Kvaratskhelia delivered a dangerous ball across Liverpool's six-yard box, allowing substitute Giovanni Simeone to tap it into the net. Giovanni, the son of Atlético de Madrid manager Diego, entered the pitch in the forty-first minute as a replacement for the injured Osimhen, and it took him only three minutes to score, adding to Liverpool's woes. Simeone's emotional celebration was understandable, as Napoli found themselves in a dreamlike scenario, leading 3-0 against Liverpool at halftime, a scoreline that didn't even flatter them considering the missed chances. The first half in Naples was one of the season's most underwhelming and subpar performances.

At halftime, Joe Gomez was substituted, with Joël Matip taking his place on the pitch. Fans couldn't help but compare Gomez's first-half display with Dejan Lovren's infamous performance against Tottenham in 2017. In both instances, the performances were woeful and rightly prompted criticism, so comparisons between the two player's performances were inevitable. Both players were substituted early to save them from their terrible performances.

Despite the substitution of Joël Matip, the team continued to struggle. Just two minutes into the second half, another goal was conceded, again highlighting the vulnerability of Liverpool's high defensive line. A long ball played over the high line found Giovanni Simeone, who managed to get behind Matip. Although Matip attempted to stop him, Simeone passed the ball across the box to Zieliński. Alisson saved Zieliński's shot, but the loose ball was not cleared as no Liverpool player was close. Zieliński followed up with a chip over Alisson, who was still on the ground after making the initial save. The brief halftime break and substitution had little impact on Liverpool's defensive struggles.

Liverpool found a consolation goal as Luis Díaz netted in the forty-ninth minute. The play started with Andy Robertson winning the ball in midfield and delivering a pass to Díaz. The wide forward showcased his skill by curling a precise low shot into the bottom corner of the net. Although Napoli's goalkeeper, Alex Meret, managed to get a slight touch on the ball, he couldn't prevent it from finding the back of the net.

This match was a complete disaster for Liverpool in every aspect. The team's performance was lifeless and uninspiring across all areas of the pitch. The attack struggled to create scoring opportunities, and the defence could not keep out the opposition's threats. There was a notable absence of fight, passion, desire, and responsibility from the players. The overall intensity and desire were sorely lacking, leaving fans disappointed and frustrated. The team lacked the desire to fight for a positive result, which was deeply concerning.

Liverpool's renowned pressing style, a critical element of their success in the recent past, had been noticeably absent. The team struggled to apply the same overwhelming pressure on their opponents as they had done in the past. Among the squad, only Luis Díaz, Harvey Elliott, and Alisson could be exempted from the criticism, as they had shown effort and commendable performances. New arrivals and injured players can be given some leniency, as they needed time to adapt or were unable to contribute from the sidelines. However, the majority of the squad had, at some point, let Liverpool down during the early stages of this season, despite it being just seven games in. The lack of consistency and underwhelming performances from crucial players told us what to expect for the rest of the season.

Jamie Carragher's description of Liverpool's high defensive line as 'Suicide football' highlighted the risk involved in such an aggressive defensive strategy. The high line and the midfield's lack of effective pressing left Liverpool's defence vulnerable and exposed. Without the midfield press, opponents could exploit the gaps and find space to make easy passes, leading to chaotic situations for Liverpool's defence. This issue was not limited to specific opponents but had become a blueprint for all teams to exploit and create problems for Liverpool.

The image of Klopp raising his hands apologetically to the fans and his apology during the post-match press conference reflected the disappointment and frustration felt by everyone associated with Liverpool. The players' performance fell short of expectations, and Klopp acknowledged that the fans deserved better. The collective sentiment was that it was time for the team to step up and deliver the level of performance that Liverpool fans have come to expect because what we saw in Naples was unacceptable.

Liverpool 2 - 1 Ajax

UEFA Champions League (Matchday 2)
Tuesday, 13th September 2022
Anfield

Liverpool responded positively in their Champions League home match against Ajax, showcasing a marked improvement from their disappointing performance in Naples. Jürgen Klopp's statement that this performance, compared to the one in Naples, was like a different sport highlighted the stark contrast between the two matches. Liverpool's performance against Ajax was much better, and this positive response reflected their ability to deliver a performance that is more in line with their capabilities.

Liverpool displayed a renewed sense of unity and determination in their performance. The players showed a collective effort and worked cohesively as a team. The lack of vulnerability from lobbed-through balls showed an improved defensive organisation, and the return of some pressing intensity indicated some level of resurgence. While the pressing wasn't flawless, it was a positive development that showed desire. The players appeared revitalised and showed no signs of fatigue, contributing to an overall improved and familiar display.

Three players stood out in this match, but there were strong performances all around. Kostas Tsimikas started at left-back and excelled in the game's attacking and defensive aspects. His contribution was vital, and he even assisted Joël Matip's crucial match-winning goal in the eighty-ninth minute through a perfectly delivered corner. Tsimikas had an excellent performance, leaving fans impressed and open to him retaining the spot in the first team. Andy Robertson was sidelined with a knee injury, and the presence of Tsimikas provided reassurance that there was no need to rush Robertson's return, as Tsimikas had shown he could fill the role effectively.

Thiago's return to Liverpool's midfield was a welcome sight, and his impact on the team was evident. His unique skill set sets him apart from other players in Liverpool's squad and the wider footballing world. He is an exceptional ball passer and can orchestrate the team's play. He has also added aggressive tackling to his game, further enhancing his contributions on the defensive side of his game. Thiago's performances can appear effortless when he is in form and fit, displaying his world-class abilities. Given his importance to the team, Liverpool needed to prioritise his well-being and protect him from injuries. While Thiago has faced criticism for his vulnerability to injuries, his performance in this match highlighted his world-class talent. It was crucial to keep him fit and performing at this high level. Unfortunately, during the later stage of the season, he experienced a hip flexor injury that forced him to miss eleven matches. However, in this game against Ajax, Thiago delivered a fantastic performance. His display served as a reminder of his world-class talent and the impact he can have when fully fit.

Another exceptional player was Joël Matip. He displayed confidence and composure throughout the match, making a strong case for retaining his position alongside Virgil in Liverpool's defence. Not only did he score the decisive goal, but he also consistently contributed to the team's attacking movements. Matip's ability to drive forward, break through Ajax's defensive lines, and create dangerous opportunities with his precise forward passes, and dribbles were impressive. In my opinion, Matip left Klopp with no alternative. He deserved to be the first-choice right-sided centre-back for the foreseeable future. However, he only started the next three games until Ibrahima Konaté took his place in the starting eleven.

Liverpool broke the deadlock with a seemingly straightforward goal. Alisson started the play by playing a long ball into the final third. Luis Díaz displayed excellent aerial ability, winning a contested header against Ajax defender Jurriën Timber. Díaz deftly flicked the ball into the path of Diogo Jota, and his presence approaching the box caused concern for two Ajax defenders, who diverted their attention away from Mohamed Salah. Having Jota as a distraction resulted in a moment of panic as the Ajax defenders attempted to close down the danger.

Consequently, Salah found himself in an advantageous position with plenty of space. Jota intelligently passed the ball to the unmarked Salah, who took a touch before unleashing a shot towards the near post, finding the back of the net.

Ajax levelled the score with a powerful strike from Mohamed Kudus inside the penalty area. The build-up to the goal involved Ajax exploiting Liverpool's right wing, prompting some fans to question Trent Alexander-Arnold's defensive efforts. While there may have been room for improvement in tracking Steven Berghuis, it was not as shocking as Trent's defending in the previous match. Joël

Matip attempted to close down Berghuis to prevent any dangerous passes or crosses across the box, but his efforts were in vain. Berghuis successfully delivered the ball into the box to Kudus, who unleashed an unstoppable shot that crashed against the underside of the crossbar, leaving Alisson with no chance of making a save.

Liverpool's improved performance and a late goal from Matip added a cheerful ending to the match. Despite some missed chances from both teams in the second half, Liverpool was the team that grabbed the winner. The victory was a welcome reward for their efforts and provided a sense of optimism for future matches.

In the eighty-ninth minute, Liverpool was awarded a corner in front of the Kop. Matip, a threat from corners all game, made contact with the ball directly from the corner kick. There was a moment of uncertainty as to whether the ball had crossed the goal line, but the referee consulted the technology on his wrist and confirmed the goal. Matip celebrated passionately with the fans in the Kop, relieved and ecstatic to secure the victory for Liverpool. The goal provided a sense of relief and joy for both the players and the supporters.

During his post-match interview with BT Sport, Virgil van Dijk had some interesting things to say. Interviewer Des Kelly said the Liverpool dressing room is full of trophy winners that will know how to correct performances, and Virgil replied:

> *Not listening to the outside world that's the most important thing. It's funny sometimes because there are a lot of ex-football players who know exactly what we go through, but they say a lot of things to try and get us down. We know last week was unacceptable. It was very, very bad. But we tried to make it right, and this is a step in the right direction.*

I don't think anyone anticipated this candid response from Virgil, but it highlighted the deep frustration he must have felt during Liverpool's difficult period. It's important to remember that players are not machines; they have emotions and feelings. When things aren't going well, criticism isn't always the most constructive approach, especially when it comes from ex-football players who should understand the difficulties of the game or journalists who have never stepped onto the pitch themselves. Virgil's comment served as a reminder that empathy and understanding can go a long way in supporting players through challenging times.

October

2022

- Brighton (H) - 1st October - EPL - Page 88

- Rangers (H) - 4th October - UCL - Page 96

- Arsenal (A) - 9th October - EPL - Page 103

- Rangers (A) - 12th October - UCL - Page 112

- Man City (H) - 16th October - EPL - Page 119

- West Ham (H) - 19th October - EPL - Page 125

- Nottm. Forrest (A) - 22nd October - EPL - Page 131

- Ajax (A) - 26th October - UCL - Page 140

- Leeds (H) - 29th October - EPL - Page 146

Liverpool 3 - 3 Brighton

Premier League
Saturday, 1st October 2022
Anfield

Postponements and an international break resulted in a twenty-eight-day gap between Liverpool's Premier League matches. While the break provided some much-needed respite for the fans from the disappointing start to the season, there was also a sense of anticipation among fans, including myself, for Liverpool's return to league action. The extended period without a game allowed the team to regroup, recharge, and address any issues or injuries they may have been facing. Well, it should have.

There was a sense of uncertainty surrounding Brighton ahead of the match due to their managerial change. Former manager Graham Potter had left Brighton to join Chelsea, and the appointment of Roberto De Zerbi as his successor introduced an element of the unknown. He was unfamiliar to Premier League audiences but had garnered attention as an up-and-coming manager. Liverpool would have had to prepare by watching footage from his previous managerial role with Shakhtar Donetsk to gain insights into his playing style and tactical approach. The managerial transition added an intriguing element to the match, raising questions about how Brighton would perform under the new manager.

Liverpool *had* to turn their form around in October, which various journalists labelled as a crucial period. It was a busy month and seen as make-or-break for The Reds. They needed to start rebuilding their campaign. However, to the disappointment of the supporters, the first match of the month ended in a draw at home to Brighton. It was frustrating at home against a team Liverpool should expect to beat. This is not meant to undermine Brighton, who have consistently been a well-managed club in recent seasons. Under De Zerbi, they continued progressing and exceeding expectations, ultimately securing a Europa League place, a wonderful success story for the club. Nevertheless, this draw meant that Liverpool dropped two more points, making climbing the Premier League table even more challenging.

There had been significant discussion surrounding Trent Alexander-Arnold in the week leading up to this match. Gareth Southgate's public comments comparing Trent to Kieran Trippier sparked a debate about Trent's inclusion in England's World Cup squad. Southgate had said he prefers

Tripier as his overall game is much better. Such discussions, and the uncertainty they created, undoubtedly impacted Trent's confidence. Regrettably, he could not channel the doubts and criticisms into a motivating performance on the pitch.

Brighton posed significant challenges for Liverpool early in the first half, repeatedly creating scoring opportunities against Liverpool's vulnerable defence. Liverpool went 2-0 down, and it could have been worse if not for Alisson's crucial saves. The first goal conceded by Liverpool was preventable. Solly March delivered a decent cross into the box, which Trent headed away. However, the ball landed just outside the eighteen-yard line, where Moisés Caicedo quickly overpowered Jordan Henderson in physicality and aerial ability. Henderson seemed to lack the determination to win the ball, almost conceding that Caicedo wanted it more and letting him have it. The loose ball fell to Alexis Mac Allister, who played a simple forward pass to Danny Welbeck. Welbeck cleverly backheeled the ball into the path of Leandro Trossard, who smoothly allowed the ball to roll across his body before unleashing a left-footed shot, leaving Trent, who was trying to recover positionally, on the floor. Although Trent slipped while trying to regain his position, the goal could have been prevented with better defensive organisation and determination from certain players.

In the lead-up to Brighton's second goal, Trent lost control of the ball while trying to chest it down. Positioned too centrally, the ball bounced off his chest and was intercepted by Danny Welbeck, who headed it out to left-wing-back Pervis Estupiñán. Although Trent tried to close down Estupiñán, he could not block the pass back to Welbeck, who made a clever run into the space behind Trent. Welbeck then played the ball to March, who was just outside the eighteen-yard line. March delivered a perfectly weighted forward pass to Trossard, who scored from a similar angle as his first goal. While Brighton deserved credit for their lead, Liverpool could have defended both goals better. After only eighteen minutes, finding themselves 2-0 down was a significant setback.

Roberto Firmino was the player who scored Liverpool's first goal, starting a comeback and providing a foundation for Liverpool to build upon after their poor start. The goal came about through a typical forward dribble and a line-breaking pass from Joël Matip, which fortunately bounced to Jordan Henderson. Henderson then played a lobbed through-ball to Mohamed Salah. Instead of confidently shooting with his left foot or chipping the ball past the onrushing Brighton goalkeeper Robert Sánchez, Salah played a blind pass across the box. Fortunately, Firmino was in the correct position to get on the end of it and score. While it's possible that there was some telepathic understanding between Salah and Firmino due to their years of playing together, it appeared more like a lucky pass rather than a precise one. Nevertheless, Liverpool had managed to reduce the deficit to 2-1 by halftime.

Luis Díaz was brought on at the beginning of the second half, replacing Fábio Carvalho, and he immediately displayed the drive and determination that Jürgen Klopp would have expected and no doubt emphasised during the halftime break. Díaz played a crucial role in Firmino's second goal, which levelled the score at 2-2. The talented Colombian winger showcased his close ball control as he dribbled into the box, eventually delivering a seemingly simple side-foot pass to Firmino, who was positioned near the penalty spot. Firmino's quick footwork caused Brighton's centre-back Lewis Dunk to lose his balance and fall to the ground, which allowed Firmino time to slot the ball into the side netting to equalise calmly.

Nine minutes after the equalising goal, Liverpool took the lead for the first time. Trent delivered a corner kick into the box, and Brighton goalkeeper Sánchez attempted to punch it away from a dangerous area. However, Sánchez misjudged the ball's flight, completely missing his punch. The ball continued its trajectory and struck Brighton defender Adam Webster, who could not react or reposition himself in time. As a result, the ball deflected into the goal, granting Liverpool the lead. While it was a fortunate goal, it completed Liverpool's comeback.

Liverpool showed character by staging a comeback from 2-0 down to take a winning position. It was a testament to their determination, which overshadowed their earlier defensive vulnerability. Securing a victory would have provided a much-needed boost, as winning matches often helps mask shortcomings. However, it proved challenging for Liverpool to keep their lead and avoid conceding another goal.

As Brighton applied increasing pressure in search of an equaliser, Liverpool's defence faced a challenging task. Alisson once again made crucial saves to keep Liverpool in the lead. However, Brighton's persistence eventually paid off with an equalising goal that *again* highlighted the vulnerability in Liverpool's defence. Exploiting the space behind Trent Alexander-Arnold had become a familiar strategy for opposing teams. This was not solely a Trent issue but rather a tactical concern within Liverpool's style of play. In the case of Brighton's equaliser, Kaoru Mitoma's cross found its way to Trossard, with Virgil van Dijk unable to clear the ball. Welbeck's lack of preparedness also played a role as the ball passed him by because he didn't expect Virgil to miss his clearance attempt. Still, Trossard capitalised on the opportunity and found the back of the net despite Alisson's best efforts to save the shot. Trossard had scored all three goals for Brighton, completing his hat trick.

After such a long wait, the disappointing performance and result left fans again disheartened and searching for answers. The uncertainty lingered, with doubts about how long this unfavourable run would persist. There was no easy solution to the challenges faced by Liverpool. The ambition of challenging for the league title was unrealistic, and even a successful cup run appeared a distant and elusive dream. Believe it or not, a winning streak of several matches felt like a far-off fantasy. As supporters waited to see what the rest of the season held, there was an underlying fear that things may worsen before they improved.

Even the most optimistic fan would find it challenging to believe Liverpool could win the Premier League from here.

As we know, with hindsight, Liverpool was far from the title race for the whole season. The obstacles ahead seemed insurmountable, even at the beginning of October. The genuine concern lay in the fact that Liverpool would struggle to secure a top-four qualifying place for the Champions League. Again, with the fullness of time, we know that Liverpool didn't finish in the top four to qualify for the Champions League, so supporter concerns *were* valid.

The next Premier League fixture against Arsenal at the Emirates Stadium posed another significant challenge for Liverpool. Arsenal had been in excellent form, making it a tough encounter. They were the only team that challenged Manchester City for the Premier League title until they faded away at the business end of the season. Given the circumstances of playing such an in-form team, some fans may have preferred another extended break from Premier League matches, akin to the previous twenty-eight days without a game. However, such luck was not on Liverpool's side, and they had to brace themselves for the ongoing grind of a challenging month in poor to average form.

Liverpool 2 - 0 Rangers

UEFA Champions League (Matchday 3)
Tuesday, 4th October 2022
Anfield

Liverpool found solace in the Champions League again, securing a comfortable victory and adding three valuable points to their tally in their quest to progress from the group stage. The win boosted the team and supporters, offering a break from their challenges in domestic competitions.

Jürgen Klopp surprised fans with a change in formation, deviating from the traditional 4-3-3 setup. This unexpected change raised eyebrows among supporters accustomed to the team's successful use of the tried and tested system in previous trophy-winning campaigns. A change was necessary as Liverpool had been lacking intensity all season. The decision to modify the formation may have been influenced by the anticipation of facing a back-five defence from Rangers. It remained to be seen whether Liverpool would persist with this new shape or revert to their familiar formation in future matches.

The anticipation of witnessing Mohamed Salah, Luis Díaz, Darwin Núñez, and Diogo Jota in the starting lineup created a sense of excitement among fans. The prospect of these talented players sharing the pitch raised hopes that a positive change was on the horizon for Liverpool. The starting lineup announcement provided optimism, fueling anticipation for the start of the match.

The introduction of Liverpool's new formation sparked a debate among fans and experts regarding its exact shape. Opinions varied; some perceived it as a 4-2-3-1 formation, while others saw it as a 4-4-2 or even a 4-2-4 system. The fluidity of formations, which often adapt to the team's attacking or defensive phases, further complicated the discussion. Fan media voices such as Neil Atkinson from The Anfield Wrap and Chris Pajak from The Redmen TV strongly believed in the 4-2-4 interpretation. Regardless, Klopp expressed satisfaction with the team's efforts during a light training session where they practised the new formation. During his pre-match interview, when asked about the change of shape, Klopp said:

We just thought we had to change, and that's what we did formation-wise. Let's see how it works out. There's never a perfect time to change. We had to change anyway. We felt it was right. We play so many games that we can't always push the same boys through, so we decided like that.

Contrary to expectations, Klopp was willing to deviate from his successful system and experiment with a new formation. This surprising decision challenged the notion of his stubbornness and demonstrated an openness to change, which felt like a breath of fresh air. While a single home win against Rangers using the new system did not indicate that all issues within the Liverpool camp had been resolved, it provided hope for the team's future. It was a positive step forward and a little reason for optimism.

In the match's early stages, a foul committed by ex-Liverpool player Ben Davies presented Trent Alexander-Arnold with an opportunity to show his set-piece ability. Determined to silence his critics, Trent executed a flawless free kick, leaving Rangers goalkeeper Allan McGregor helpless as the ball gracefully found its way into the top left corner of the net. Trent attempted to maintain composed during his celebration, but his emotions broke through as his teammates engulfed him in jubilation.

Liverpool dominated Rangers in all areas of the field, showing their suffocating and relentless attacking approach. It was a refreshing sight after their recent struggles. Darwin Núñez, although unable to find the back of the net, delivered an impressive performance in a Liverpool shirt. The change in dynamics was noticeable with Núñez constantly playing on the last defender's shoulder, a departure from Firmino's usual false nine role.

It is essential to acknowledge the outstanding performance of Allan McGregor, the Rangers goalkeeper, in this match. Despite facing relentless pressure from Liverpool, McGregor displayed exceptional goalkeeping and made several impressive saves, particularly in his battle with Darwin Núñez. McGregor's contributions were instrumental in preventing Rangers from suffering a more significant defeat.

For Liverpool's second goal, Jordan Henderson displayed his vision and passing ability by delivering a long ball to Luis Díaz on the left wing. Díaz, upon receiving the ball, immediately took on the Rangers' defence with his impressive dribbling skills. His dynamic run caused chaos and forced the Rangers' defenders to bring him down inside the penalty area, resulting in a penalty. Mohamed Salah stepped up to take the penalty and confidently struck the ball down the middle, beating the goalkeeper and extending Liverpool's lead to 2-0.

Despite Rangers' limited opportunities, there was a moment of danger when Rabbi Matondo found space behind Trent Alexander-Arnold and managed to get past Joël Matip to deliver a cross into Liverpool's six-yard box. However, Kostas Tsimikas showed great awareness and commitment by clearing the ball before it could reach Fashion Sakala, who would have had a simple tap-in. Tsimikas's heroic clearance made him tumble into the net, but he showed determination to protect Liverpool's lead. Tsimikas' clearance led to a Rangers corner, and Antonio Čolak had a chance to score at the back post. However, Alisson came to Liverpool's rescue, making himself big and producing a crucial save to prevent a potentially nervy ending to the match.

Liverpool's new formation and tactical approach brought a refreshing fluidity to their attacking play. The four attacking players constantly rotated their positions, causing uncertainty and confusion within the Rangers' defence. This dynamic movement made it difficult for Rangers to anticipate Liverpool's next move and mark their attacking threats effectively. Furthermore, the defensive structure of Liverpool appeared more organised and solid. Trent Alexander-Arnold's slightly less attacking role provided better defensive cover, reducing the space behind him for Rangers to exploit. The presence of Jordan Henderson and Thiago in midfield added an extra layer of protection for Liverpool's back line, effectively shielding them from any potential threats. However, It is worth noting that Rangers struggled to make an impact in the attacking third, which can be attributed to Liverpool's improved defensive setup but mostly because of Rangers' limited attacking opportunities. The attacking momentum graph for this match showed Liverpool's dominance throughout the match, showing their ability to maintain possession, create scoring opportunities, and limit the opposition's chances. It was about as one-sided as a match can be.

Liverpool's victory against Rangers felt crucial for their campaign. While it was important not to undermine Rangers' abilities, the match allowed Liverpool to experiment and adapt their playing style in a somewhat competitive environment. The outcome of the other Group A fixture, with Napoli defeating Ajax, further emphasised the significance of Liverpool's win. It propelled them into second position in the group standings, positioning them favourably for qualification to the competition's knockout stage.

Everything feels much better after a win, and it's easy to take it for granted when Liverpool is consistently performing at their best and securing victories week after week. This is what I learnt about this season. Enjoy it When Liverpool wins because it is miserable when Liverpool isn't in winning form.

Arsenal 3 - 2 Liverpool

Premier League
Sunday, 9th October 2022
Emirates Stadium

Albert Einstein defined insanity as doing the same thing repeatedly and expecting different results. As a Liverpool supporter, it is frustrating when the team continues to struggle with the same issues and the same players underperform without any signs of improvement. This season, Liverpool has been Einstein's definition of insanity.

Liverpool's league form up to and including this match had been abysmal, leaving everyone wondering why a team that challenged for multiple trophies was now struggling to secure a top-four position. Speculations and theories from journalists and fans had yet to provide concrete answers. The reasons behind Liverpool's sudden decline remained unknown, which led to plenty of speculation. Their league form was a catastrophic failure that only improved towards the end of the season.

Arsenal displayed an impressive performance and showed their determination, passion, and attacking prowess, fully deserving the victory. Their well-organised team shape and understanding demonstrated a clear game plan and identity throughout the match. As a result, the three points rightfully went to the North London side. On the other hand, Liverpool fell short and did not deserve any points from the game, as they lacked drive and failed to match Arsenal's performance.

Fans anticipated which formation Liverpool would employ against this in-form Arsenal team. Whether they would return to the familiar 4-3-3 or maintain the new formation from the previous victory against Rangers. Surprisingly, Jürgen Klopp opted to continue with the successful formation from midweek. While it was a bold decision, it ultimately proved irrelevant as the team's fundamentals were lacking.

Despite the improved defensive stability showcased by the formation change in the previous match, Liverpool's hopes of maintaining that solidity were shattered within the first minute. In a disappointing turn of events, Arsenal swiftly capitalised on a defensive lapse, taking an early 1-0 lead. Bukayo Saka delivered a well-placed pass to Martin Ødegaard, and although Jordan Henderson had an opportunity to intercept the pass, he didn't do so effectively. Ødegaard then executed a perfect through ball between Trent Alexander-Arnold and Joël Matip, finding Gabriel Martinelli, who had made a well-timed run. Martinelli wasted no time, striking the ball past an advancing Alisson. Liverpool found themselves trailing by a goal just one minute into the match, a familiar tale that had haunted this season.

Before Liverpool's equaliser, there was a contentious moment when Liverpool had a penalty shout turned down by referee Michael Oliver. Diogo Jota attempted to play the ball across the box, which struck Gabriel Magalhães' hand, which was positioned unnaturally beside his shoulder. Gary Neville, providing co-commentary, initially believed that the ball had made contact with Gabriel's hand when watching it live. However, as VAR reviewed the incident and replays were shown, Neville expressed his belief that Gabriel could be in trouble. Despite these observations, no penalty was awarded by the on-field referee. Dermot Gallagher, a former referee who analyses refereeing decisions through Sky Sports' segment Ref Watch, expressed his surprise that VAR did not recommend Michael Oliver to review the incident on the pitchside screen.

Liverpool's equaliser came not long after the penalty incident. Trent Alexander-Arnold played a lofted through ball over the Arsenal defence, and Gabriel's attempted clearance fell into the path of Luis Díaz. Díaz quickly headed the ball forward, allowing him to run onto it and deliver a well-placed cross into the box. Darwin Núñez, stretching to reach the cross, made contact with the ball, which went past Arsenal goalkeeper Aaron Ramsdale and found the back of the net. Liverpool had successfully bounced back from conceding the opening goal, gaining more momentum as the first half progressed. However, just before halftime, a moment of inexplicable madness resulted in Liverpool conceding again.

In the dying moments of the first half, with Liverpool in possession from a deep set piece, the centre-backs ventured forward in search of another goal. Kostas Tsimikas delivered a high ball up the pitch, headed down by Joël Matip about twenty yards from the goal. However, Liverpool's attacking free-kick quickly became trouble as Arsenal initiated a quick counter-attack. Thiago had a chance to make a professional foul on Gabriel Martinelli but inexplicably chose not to do so. Martinelli passed the ball to Gabriel Jesus, creating a three-on-three situation, with Martin Ødegaard pushing hard to make it a four-on-three advantage for Arsenal. As Martinelli dribbled down Arsenal's left wing, Trent Alexander-Arnold had a moment of utter stupidity by abandoning his central position to press the ball. This decision was even more baffling as Martinelli had not evaded Jordan Henderson's defensive efforts. Despite Henderson's commendable attempt to keep pace with the faster Martinelli and stop or slow Arsenal's attack, Trent's brainless move left a gaping hole in the centre of Liverpool's defence.

Martinelli cleverly halted his run, deceiving Henderson and Trent, who was effectively neutralised because of his sudden halt. With Martinelli now facing a three-versus-one situation, only Tsimikas remained, and he was helpless in this scenario. The ball eventually found its way to Bukayo Saka at the back post, who tapped it in, giving Arsenal a 2-1 lead seconds before the halftime whistle blew.

It can only be described as a series of idiotic and calamitous errors by players who should have known better. Using hindsight and knowing Liverpool conceded from their own attacking free-kick makes assessing the situation seem more straightforward, but why were the centre-backs going up for a deep free-kick so late in the first half when there was always the possibility of Arsenal springing a quick counter-attack? Why didn't Thiago take down Gabriel Martinelli when he had the chance? Why did Trent leave the centre position, vacating a massive space to close down Martinelli, whom

Henderson was still marking? It was moments before halftime, and it all could have been stopped if Liverpool had an ounce of game awareness–unforgivable stupidity.

The second half brought hope for Liverpool as substitute Roberto Firmino scored a superb goal to level the score. Firmino made a well-timed run behind William Saliba, and Diogo Jota played a precise through-ball to find him. Firmino's first touch allowed him to continue his momentum into the box, and he precisely struck the ball into the far bottom corner. It was a great goal from the Brazilian, and credit goes to Jota for seeing his run. However, it is deeply frustrating to witness moments of brilliance like this, knowing that Liverpool is still capable of them, only to be undone by their own foolishness and avoidable errors.

Firmino's substitution into the match resulted from Luis Díaz's unfortunate injury towards the end of the first half. Losing Díaz, an energetic and influential player for Liverpool, was a blow the team could not afford. The club confirmed that Díaz's recovery would extend beyond the World Cup, effectively ruling him out for the remainder of the calendar year. Fortunately, Colombia did not qualify for the World Cup, sparing him the disappointment of missing out on representing his country in a major tournament.

Nevertheless, it remained disheartening news for both Díaz and Liverpool.

Liverpool's defensive lapses continued to haunt them as they conceded a penalty, compounding their troubles in the match. The events leading to the penalty were filled with poor decision-making and defensive errors. Thiago's attempt to dribble past Saka in his box resulted in a loss of possession, leaving many questioning his judgment. Saka managed to get a shot off, but Alisson made a save. However, Fabinho's lacklustre clearance only reached Martinelli at the edge of the box, prolonging the danger. Martinelli took a shot that Henderson blocked, but the ball fell back to Martinelli, who passed it wide to Granit Xhaka. Xhaka then delivered a cross into the box, where Gabriel Jesus and Thiago contested for the ball. Unfortunately, Thiago made slight contact with Jesus's calf, prompting the referee to award a penalty. It was a soft decision, but it could have been avoided if Liverpool had decisively cleared the ball earlier. Saka stepped up to take the penalty and successfully converted, putting Arsenal in the lead for the third time in the match. This time, they managed to hold onto their advantage until the final whistle, leaving Liverpool with another disappointing result.

Klopp decided to turn his back and not watch the Arsenal penalty, which was apt, as I'm sure he would have liked to have turned his back on Liverpool's poor defending too. The missed opportunities to clear the ball and regain defensive shape highlighted the importance of making the correct choices and recognising threats.

Liverpool's position after this defeat left the Reds trailing league-leaders Arsenal by fourteen points, which highlighted their struggles this season. The inconsistency in their performances had been a recurring issue. Despite occasional glimpses of improvement, Liverpool struggled to maintain a consistent level and often found themselves conceding early goals. This stage of the season was crucial, as it would either provide an opportunity for Liverpool to rebuild and salvage their campaign or further compound their difficulties. The relentless nature of the fixtures meant that being in good form during this period was vital for turning things around. However, Liverpool failed to address their issues and continued to underperform, and the damage worsened.

The result between Arsenal and Liverpool certainly sparked discussions about the state of both clubs. Some could see a symbolic passing of the torch, with Arsenal on the rise and Liverpool seemingly at the end of its cycle.

Understandably, this narrative gained traction, given Arsenal's consistent performances and growing confidence. The upcoming break for the World Cup would provide supporters with a welcome break from this Jekyll and Hyde Liverpool team.

Rangers 1 - 7 Liverpool

UEFA Champions League (Matchday 4)
Wednesday, 12th October 2022
Ibrox Stadium

There is a rare and unique moment that sometimes occurs in football. It's the moment when the outcome is practically assured, and fans can bask in the knowledge that their team is on the path to victory. Liverpool supporters had limited opportunities to savour such moments this season, making them all the more valuable when they do occur.

It wasn't *all* comfortable, however. Rangers took the lead with a well-executed goal from Scott Arfield, and while Alisson couldn't have done much to save the shot, Fábio Carvalho's role in conceding possession that led to the goal left room for improvement. Ibrox understandably erupted as the home fans celebrated. From a Liverpool perspective, there was a sense of "Here we go again," recalling past matches where the team faced similar problems after conceding the first goal. However, Rangers' lead lasted seven minutes before Liverpool wrestled back the scoreline.

During a corner kick delivered by Kostas Tsimikas, Roberto Firmino engaged in a physical duel with Rangers defender James Tavernier. Both players were locked in a grabbing match, fighting for position to get a decisive header on the ball. It was a test of strength and determination. In this contest, Firmino emerged victorious, overpowering Tavernier to connect with the ball and guide it into the net. His well-executed header resulted in a relatively straightforward goal, levelling the score just before halftime.

Earlier in the evening, Napoli had emerged victorious against Ajax in the other Group A fixture. This outcome added significance to Liverpool's clash with Rangers, as a win would create a six-point gap between them and Ajax in third place. Such a lead would put Liverpool in a favourable position, needing only a single point from their remaining two matches to secure qualification to the last sixteen. However, their immediate focus was on overcoming the challenge presented by Rangers and securing the much-needed victory to solidify their position in the group.

Eight minutes into the second half, Firmino showcased his scoring prowess again, securing his second goal to give Liverpool the lead. It all began with a well-executed defensive header by Ibrahima Konaté, directing the ball towards Harvey

Elliott, who displayed brilliant awareness by flicking the ball into the path of Joe Gomez. Despite playing out of position at right-back due to Trent Alexander-Arnold's injury, Gomez went on a skilful dribble up the right wing, taking advantage of the open space on the field. He precisely delivered a low cross into the box, finding Firmino perfectly positioned. The Brazilian made no mistake, striking the ball into the back of the net. Although Rangers' goalkeeper, Allan McGregor, managed to get a foot to Firmino's shot, its power proved too much to prevent the goal.

Liverpool swiftly added a third goal shortly after. Fábio Carvalho showed his vision by playing an intelligent pass to Firmino, who showed extraordinary skill with a Rabona-style flick as his first touch, setting up Darwin Núñez perfectly. With composure, Núñez placed the ball into the far corner of the net, leaving McGregor helpless to stop it. It was a composed finish from the Uruguayan striker, highlighting his goal-scoring precision, and Firmino's contribution added a touch of class to the play.

Mohamed Salah was brought onto the pitch as a substitute in the sixty-eighth minute. Typically Salah is a guaranteed starter. However, he had struggled to meet his high expectations since returning from the AFCON final, where

Senegal defeated Egypt in February 2022. It had been clear that Salah's form had been subpar for some time, so being benched for this match motivated him to reignite his and Liverpool's season. The fact that he achieved the fastest hat trick in Champions League history as a substitute proves that he is still a player of world-class calibre. This was the Mohamed Salah that Liverpool needed desperately.

Salah's first goal was a display of exceptional skill. As the ball descended, he showed great control to bring it down perfectly. Despite being surrounded by Rangers' defenders in a confined space, Salah's close ball control enabled him to unleash a shot from a tight angle. McGregor managed to get a hand to the ball, but it was not enough to prevent it from finding the back of the net. It was a moment of individual brilliance from Salah, demonstrating his magical ball control and composure.

In contrast to his first goal, Salah's second goal resulted from excellent teamwork and coordination. It started with Thiago intercepting a clearance from the Rangers' defence, initiating a quick passing sequence. Thiago exchanged a one-two pass with Fabinho before playing a forward pass to Diogo Jota. Jota, while turning, swiftly passed the ball to Salah—the entire sequence involved one-touch passes, showing the fluid and dynamic play of Liverpool's attacking play. Salah, who had awareness and composure, controlled the ball effortlessly. Upon seeing McGregor's poor positioning, Salah calmly slotted the ball into the space left by the Rangers' goalkeeper. It was a well-executed team goal.

Salah's third goal was another classic display of his goal-scoring ability. Jota's excellent ball control and pass set up Salah, who positioned himself intelligently on the right side of the penalty area. Rather than being confined to the touchline like a traditional winger, Salah received the ball and showed his dribbling skills again, taking a few touches as he moved into the penalty area. With finesse, he curled a low shot into the far corner of the goal. This goal and his previous two emphasised the impact Salah can have when playing a more central role. Playing him as a wide winger that stretches the field limits his output and doesn't fully utilise his abilities. The remarkable six-minute hat trick undoubtedly highlighted to Klopp and the coaching staff the need to position Salah in a more central area to maximise his effectiveness.

Salah then showed his playmaking abilities for Liverpool's final goal by delivering a low cross across the box to Jota. Although Jota's first touch wasn't ideal and allowed McGregor to make a tackle, the ball fell to Harvey Elliott, who quickly fired a first-time shot into the net. Initially, the linesman raised his flag, creating a moment of uncertainty. However, VAR intervened to review the decision, and during this moment, Salah expressed his support by hugging Elliott from behind. After a brief wait, VAR confirmed that the goal was valid, leading to jubilant celebrations as Elliott had scored his first Champions League goal for Liverpool.

During a rare English interview with UEFA, Roberto Firmino was asked about Salah's record-breaking hat trick:

Amazing. When he scored the first goal, I told Darwin on the bench, 'He will score a hat-trick one hundred percent.' I could feel it on the bench, and that's exactly what he did, and I'm so happy for him.

Salah's aggression and determination were evident when he stepped onto the pitch. His desire to make an impact and prove himself was translated into a sensational performance. Darwin Núñez's composed finish showcased his budding confidence and ability to contribute to the team's goals. Harvey Elliott's performance on the right side of the midfield showed his versatility and how he can contribute effectively to Liverpool's midfield workload. Diogo Jota's hat-trick of assists for Salah's goals highlighted his creativity and understanding of his teammates' movements. Roberto Firmino's contribution of two goals and an assist underlined his importance to the team and raised intriguing questions about his future.

Liverpool's victory provided a welcome respite from their struggles in the league. Everything feels better after an emphatic victory. However, Klopp's statement post-match about not being in the title race reflected the team's poor form and distance from the league leaders. In the Champions League, however, Liverpool's position in their group was promising, with just one more point needed to secure qualification to the knockout stages.

Liverpool 1 - 0 Manchester City

Premier League
Sunday 16th October 2022
Anfield

This win against Manchester City not only bought joy during a challenging period but also carried significant weight because of the level of the opposition. The victory held the potential to be a pivotal moment in Liverpool's season, reigniting their form and reigniting hopes for future success. It proved the team still had resilience and determination when they chose to show it, and it proved that they could compete at the highest level when required.

The discussion on social media before the match was filled with criticism and scepticism. The absence of Ibrahima Konaté due to injury forced Joe Gomez to take his place alongside Virgil van Dijk at centre-back. Many assumed that Gomez would be deployed as a right-back, considering Trent Alexander-Arnold's injury. However, with Trent only fit enough for the bench and Gomez covering the centre, James

Milner was chosen to fill the right-back position. This unexpected decision sparked an uproar among fans, with some already conceding defeat to Manchester City before the game started. The adverse reaction on social media reflected the doubts and concerns surrounding Liverpool's lineup.

Ironically, it could be argued that James Milner and Joe Gomez were Liverpool's standout performers in the match. Despite his age, Milner delivered an exceptional performance, setting the standard for the team. He effectively neutralised the threat of Phil Foden, who is fourteen years his junior and kept him quiet throughout the match. Milner's experience, defensive discipline, and tactical awareness were fully displayed.

On the other hand, Joe Gomez had a perfect game, showcasing his defensive composure throughout the ninety minutes. Gomez only had a few standout performances throughout the season, but this was one of them. He consistently made crucial interceptions, tackles, and clearances, stopping Manchester City's attacking threats. Gomez's solid performance earned him the recognition he deserved, as he was awarded the Player of the Match award. Milner and Gomez's contributions were vital to Liverpool's victory in the game, demonstrating their value and impact on the team's overall performance.

The first half was a closely contested battle between the two teams, with both sides unable to find a breakthrough. The most promising opportunity arose when Kevin de Bruyne delivered an accurate cross to Erling Haarland, whose header was directed straight at Alisson. While Liverpool had their fair share of scoring chances, the match truly ignited in the second half.

Mohamed Salah found himself in a one-on-one situation against Ederson. The Brazilian goalkeeper made a crucial intervention, managing to graze Salah's shot and divert it just wide of the post by the narrowest of margins. The replay highlighted the significance of Ederson's touch, as it prevented what would have been a certain goal. Surprisingly, the referee did not award a corner to Liverpool, as the faint touch went unnoticed. The replay clearly showed that Ederson had made contact with the ball, indicating that it should have been a Liverpool corner. However, VAR could not overturn the decision, as it was not considered a clear error that warranted VAR intervention. This sequence of events left many bewildered, as the video assistant referee had access to the replays but could not instruct the on-field referee,

Anthony Taylor, to award a corner instead of a goal kick. Isn't it baffling that referees were sitting in front of a screen, carefully reviewing replays, in direct communication with the on-field referee, and could not provide any input or correction? Madness.

VAR came to Liverpool's rescue after a controversial incident where Manchester City scored a goal. Alisson was furious, claiming to have had firm control of the ball before Haaland kicked it out of his hands. VAR intervened, not for the Haarland challenge on Alisson, but for Haaland's earlier foul on Fabinho. The Norwegian striker had held Fabinho's shirt, causing him to be brought down while in possession of the ball. After reviewing the incident on the pitch-side screen, Anthony Taylor overturned the goal due to the foul on Fabinho. Pep Guardiola was visibly upset and responded by gesturing towards the Anfield crowd and shouting 'This Is Anfield' in a pathetically immature manner as if to explain that the venue and the home crowd influenced the disallowed goal decision.

Moments later, Liverpool had a promising goalscoring opportunity. Harvey Elliott threaded a well-timed pass to Diogo Jota, but João Cancelo's solid defending and recovery caused the ball to become loose. In a swift reaction, Salah seized the loose ball at the edge of the box and delivered a sublime outside-of-the-boot pass to Jota at the back post. Jota's header, unfortunately, narrowly sailed over the crossbar. Salah's pass was genuinely exceptional, showcasing his world-class vision and precision. It was a pity that Jota couldn't convert the chance, as Salah's pass deserved to be celebrated as a world-class assist, not just a world-class pass.

The chances continued to flow, with Haaland having another opportunity to find the back of the net. İlkay Gündoğan played a pass to him just outside the box, and Haaland swiftly unleashed a shot that forced Alisson to react quickly. The Liverpool goalkeeper dove to his right and made a strong-handed save, ensuring the ball stayed out of the net. It was a crucial piece of goalkeeping, keeping Liverpool in the game at a critical moment.

Salah was the player who broke the deadlock, providing a moment of brilliance for Liverpool. It all started with a Manchester City free kick, played into the box by De Bruyne. Alisson, unchallenged, collected the ball and quickly spotted an opportunity. With a perfectly executed long ball up the pitch, Alisson found Salah in space, bypassing Manchester City's defence. Salah rolled past Cancelo, the last man, leaving him one-on-one with Ederson. Displaying his finesse, Salah deftly lifted the ball over Ederson to give Liverpool the 1-0 lead. It was another glimpse of Alisson's awareness, quick thinking, and accurate long passing, and Salah's body control and clinical finishing resulted in a great goal for Liverpool.

The drama continued to unfold as Jürgen Klopp could not contain his frustration. There was a moment of controversy when Bernardo Silva brought down Salah, but to Klopp's dismay, neither the linesman nor the referee signalled a foul. Recognising the infringement, Klopp made his dissatisfaction known as the linesman hurriedly ran towards the Liverpool dugout to keep up with the play. Anthony Taylor, the referee, approached the Liverpool dugout, and in response to Klopp's angry protests, he showed the manager a red card. Klopp reluctantly retreated to the dressing room, only rejoining his team on the pitch once the final whistle had blown.

The impressive Liverpool win had to end on a sour note. Sadly, Diogo Jota suffered a late-match injury that overshadowed this victory. After requiring a stretcher to leave the pitch, subsequent scans revealed a significant injury in his calf that sidelined him for one hundred and sixteen days, during which he missed eighteen matches and the chance to represent Portugal at the World Cup held in Qatar.

Liverpool 1 - 0 West Ham Utd.

Premier League
Wednesday, 19th October 2022
Anfield

Liverpool had to grind it out for this victory. A few matches ago, I reflected on the unique feeling in football when fans, and even the players to some extent, can relax and enjoy the game, knowing that victory is all but assured due to a comfortable scoreline. However, a 1-0 scoreline is the complete opposite. It breeds anxiety because a single goal can completely alter the outcome. If the opposing team manages to equalise, they gain momentum, turning the match into a level contest, which makes a 1-0 lead incredibly precarious. Liverpool had to battle their way to the final whistle, putting in a hard-fought effort to secure all three points.

While a 1-0 victory is always appreciated, watching when a single goal can sway the entire result can be nerve-wracking. West Ham had their fair share of chances, making it far from a comfortable match for Liverpool. West Ham will likely feel disappointed that they didn't secure at least a draw, especially considering their solid second-half performance.

In the match's early stages, Alisson's misplaced passes presented West Ham with opportunities to score, and West Ham will be disappointed that they couldn't capitalise on those gifted chances. However, apart from those moments, West Ham struggled to make an impact in the first half. Their sleek one-touch control and quick one-touch passing were displayed once Liverpool found their rhythm and settled into the game. During these moments, Liverpool truly shines, showing their best football. The team's performances are often at their peak when they can execute this precise and efficient two-touch style of play. One touch to control, one touch to pass.

Darwin Núñez showcased his tenacity during the match, constantly pressing West Ham's defensive line while showing a willingness to contribute defensively. In his post-match interview, Jürgen Klopp expressed his satisfaction, stating that Núñez had now fully acclimated to the team, which with hindsight, might seem a little too soon to say. However, his confidence was growing, and being Liverpool's sole goalscorer and match-winner would have undoubtedly enhanced his confidence.

Darwin Núñez had a promising opportunity before his eventual goal. Thiago played a well-executed long ball, finding Núñez, who had made a well-timed run behind the West Ham defence. Núñez showed his instinct for first-time volleys, unleashing a shot from outside the box that forced a save from the West Ham goalkeeper, Łukasz Fabiański.

As for his actual goal, Núñez demonstrated his ability to find space between defenders as he met Kostas Tsimikas' cross with a well-timed header. The ball was directed into the ground, bouncing up and out of Fabiański's reach, resulting in a well-executed goal from the powerful centre-forward.

Núñez's impact on the game was undeniable as he continued to create chances for himself. Another ferocious volley from outside the box saw him, unfortunately, hit the post. He also showed tenacity by recovering the ball from the last defender and forcing Fabiański into a save with his subsequent shot. With each performance, Núñez's quality was becoming more clear.

However, as with any player, Núñez is not immune to criticism. Fans of rival teams still attempt to undermine his abilities by comparing him to lesser strikers or labelling him as a waste of money. These baseless comments are often fueled by jealousy or a desire to see Liverpool fail.

Fortunately, such criticisms hold no weight, and I have complete confidence in Núñez's abilities. Under the guidance of one of the best coaches in football, Jürgen Klopp, there is no doubt that he will eventually flourish and prove his worth for Liverpool.

West Ham started to assert themselves towards the end of the first half, creating a few half-chances that Liverpool's defence managed to handle. However, their breakthrough came when Flynn Downes delivered a flicked ball into the penalty area, finding Jarrod Bowen. Unfortunately, Joe Gomez's attempt to win the ball was an unnecessary and mistimed challenge. In hindsight, Gomez must have been disappointed with his decision-making. Bowen controlled the ball with his chest, moving away from the goal without posing an immediate threat. However, Gomez decided to challenge, and it was clumsy, making contact with Bowen in the box.

Initially, the referee didn't award a foul, but VAR intervened and asked the on-field referee to review the incident on the pitch-side screen. After a short review, Stuart Attwell decided to award a penalty. During this pause in play, there was footage of Virgil van Dijk grinding his heel into the penalty spot, which some criticised as unsportsmanlike conduct. It's hard to argue against, as Virgil's action was an attempt to make the penalty kick more challenging for Bowen, the West Ham penalty taker. Nevertheless, Bowen stepped up to take the penalty, but Alisson came to Liverpool's rescue with a fantastic diving save, pushing the ball out of danger. Alisson's heroics ensured that Liverpool went into halftime with the game still level.

The second half proved to be an intense and competitive affair, with both teams having their fair share of opportunities. Liverpool came close to extending their lead through Curtis Jones and Roberto Firmino, while West Ham's Kurt Zouma had a nervy moment when his clearance struck the top of the crossbar, almost resulting in an own goal.

West Ham had chances too. A high-lobbed ball from Declan Rice into the box found Saïd Benrahma at the back post, but his resulting shot was tame and easily collected by Alisson. However, their most significant chance came late in the match. Benrahma played a precise pass to Bowen in the box, whose close control and quick feet allowed him to set up Tomáš Souček for what seemed like a certain goal. Just as Souček was about to shoot, James Milner made a crucial and well-timed lunge, getting a toe to the ball and preventing a late equaliser. The ball ricocheted off Alisson's legs as he dived to save the anticipated Souček shot, resulting in a baffling moment that didn't end with a goal. Liverpool was fortunate to escape conceding.

Securing a victory against West Ham was crucial, especially after the significant win against Manchester City. Failing to claim all three points would have diminished the impact of their previous victory. Fortunately, Liverpool managed to emerge victorious despite the precarious scoreline being challenging to watch. Ultimately, what mattered most was that they got the job done and secured the valuable three points.

There were seven fixtures left for Liverpool before the World Cup in Qatar: four Premier League matches, two Champions League matches, and one in the Carabao Cup. The hope was for Liverpool to emerge victorious in all of these games. Even if the wins were hard-fought 1-0 results, I was willing to endure them for the sake of Liverpool's points tally. Sadly, it didn't work out that way.

Nottm. Forest 1 - 0 Liverpool

Premier League
Saturday 22nd October 2022
City Ground

Hello Mr. Hyde. It has been a while. Well, thirteen days, to be exact. Thirteen days since the loss to Arsenal, and here you are again, uninvited. I thought we had lost you when we turned the corner. We didn't turn the corner at all, did we? Because here you are, once again.

Liverpool Football Club reverted to their less favoured alter ego again, displaying a subpar performance in their match against Nottingham Forest. This performance was awful and is among the most disappointing ones we witnessed this season.

A noticeable pattern was starting to emerge in Liverpool's defeats, including losses against Napoli, Manchester United, Arsenal, and Nottingham Forest. All of these losses have one common factor: they were away fixtures. For context, Liverpool's only away victory at this point in the season came against Rangers at Ibrox in the Champions League.

Furthermore, their results at Craven Cottage and Goodison Park, both draws, also contributed to their underwhelming away form in the Premier League.

There was a sense of déjà vu as more players were sidelined with knocks and injuries. Notably, Darwin Núñez and Thiago could not join the squad for the match in Nottingham. The decision was made to avoid risking Núñez, who had sustained a minor muscle injury in the West Ham victory. Thiago, on the other hand, was absent due to an ear infection. In his post-match interview, Jürgen Klopp confirmed that Thiago had experienced pain when he woke up at 5 am. After a visit to the hospital, Thiago returned home to rest. As a result, Curtis Jones was responsible for filling Thiago's position in the starting eleven.

In previous entries in this book, I expressed concerns regarding the squad's management, particularly in sports science and general well-being. The lack of care and responsibility had been disheartening and borderline neglectful. The increasing number of injured players is a clear indication of this mismanagement. Darwin Núñez's absence further highlighted the issue.

Twenty-three players missed at least one match, almost every player in the twenty-six-man squad. Considering that these twenty-three players have collectively sat out a staggering three hundred and eight games, the issue's magnitude becomes clear. This extensive list of absences raises serious questions about the team's overall fitness levels and the effectiveness of injury prevention measures. It highlights the desperate need for a thorough evaluation of the club's medical and sports science practices to identify shortcomings and develop better strategies to reduce the frequency and severity of injuries.

Liverpool must prioritise player well-being to sustain consistent performance and achieve long-term success. By addressing these concerns, the club can build a healthier and more resilient squad capable of enduring the season's demands and maintaining its competitive edge. Liverpool must sign robust players. After all, the best ability is availability.

I don't want to undermine Nottingham Forest's performance. They executed their game plan effectively. While they may not have been exceptional, they capitalised on their opportunities. If Liverpool had performed at their best, they would have beaten Forest and secured a comfortable victory. The reality is that Forest didn't have to exert extra effort to defeat Liverpool. They took their goal-scoring opportunity and emerged victorious. Liverpool's underwhelming performance, with a lack of effectiveness in the final third, a passive midfield, and lacking defensive solidity and confidence, contributed to their downfall.

Harvey Elliott tried to spark Liverpool into life by actively seeking the ball and attempting to begin attacks. However, apart from Elliott's efforts, Liverpool lacked forward passes that could penetrate the opposition's defence and provide opportunities for Mohamed Salah and Roberto Firmino. Salah, in particular, had limited involvement in the match due to a lack of service in dangerous areas. Upon reviewing Salah's player statistics, it is evident that his impact was minimal. He completed only four passes, failed to win any of his five ground duels, and had four shots with only two on target, both of which lacked power. Furthermore, Salah lost possession nine times. It is worth noting that Salah sustained an injury during the first half, although there was no apparent contact. Despite the injury, Salah continued to play, but it could have affected his performance on the pitch.

Liverpool had several chances to score, particularly from set pieces where Virgil van Dijk had opportunities to head the ball into the net. However, rather than taking a direct shot, Virgil headed back across the box to create a scoring chance for a teammate. Unfortunately, on two occasions, no Liverpool player was in the correct position to capitalise on the situation. It was unclear whether this was a tactical decision made before the match or a spontaneous choice by Virgil. Regardless, it proved ineffective and prevented Liverpool from converting those chances into goals.

Adding to the disappointment, Liverpool conceded a goal that could have been avoided, which was a recurring theme. The sequence leading to the goal started when former Liverpool player Taiwo Awoniyi dispossessed Joe Gomez near the halfway line. As Awoniyi looked to break away, Gomez had to stop his progress by committing a professional foul, resulting in a yellow card. At this point, it was not a catastrophic situation for Liverpool. However, the real blow came when Nottingham Forest capitalised on the deep free kick and found the back of the net. At least Gomez had some game awareness and committed a professional foul, it was the right thing to do, and we don't see enough Liverpool players act this way. The players can be too nice.

Morgan Gibbs-White delivered the set piece, lofting the ball towards the right side of the penalty area. Steve Cook controlled the ball with a good touch and unleashed a powerful half-volley, directing it low and towards the far side of the box. Despite Virgil's attempt to intercept the ball, he failed to make contact, allowing it to reach Taiwo Awoniyi. Awoniyi's initial shot struck the post, but the rebound fell kindly to him, and he made no mistake in slotting it into the empty net. Alisson remained grounded after his initial dive, unable to make a save.

Alisson continued to play a crucial role for Liverpool, making vital saves to prevent a more severe and humiliating defeat. His determination, desire, and exceptional abilities have made him a standout performer. Given his outstanding contributions, Alisson was the sole contender for Liverpool's Player of the Season award. In June 2022, Alisson won the Standard Charted Player of the Season award, and rightly so.

However, it was uncomfortable to witness Alisson venturing forward for late corners. Considering it was only October, it felt embarrassing. While the high stakes justified Alisson's involvement in previous situations, like the all-important goal against West Brom to help secure a Champions League spot, the question was: did Liverpool find themselves in a similarly critical battle for a top-four position in October? It is not a criticism of Alisson but rather an acknowledgement that relying on him to join the attack in such circumstances reflects the team's desperation.

Assuming Liverpool used a 4-4-2 formation against Nottingham Forest, the midfield quartet from left to right comprised Fábio Carvalho, Curtis Jones, Fabinho, and Harvey Elliott. I do not want to sound pessimistic or defeatist, but that midfield four was not good enough even for a match against Forest. Liverpool had a handful of midfield injuries, which may explain the fringe player selections. However, the lack of investment in the midfield area was worrying, and this season is truly starting to show the flaws in Liverpool and FSG's transfer policy.

Liverpool showed interest in Aurélien Tchouaméni during the 2022 summer transfer window, but the player ultimately chose to join Real Madrid. While it is true that Liverpool has established itself as a top club, it is essential to note that the club's recruitment strategy prioritises players who are considered the right fit for the team's style, philosophy, and long-term plans. This approach has proven successful, as seen with the signings of players like Andy Robertson, Georginio Wijnaldum, and Xherdan Shaqiri, who joined Liverpool from clubs relegated from the Premier League. These players have made significant contributions to Liverpool's success.

However, Liverpool is *against* signing these types of players now, as if these types of signings are somehow beneath them because of their success. It's an elitist and almost arrogant attitude only to consider the best players. If these players opt to go elsewhere, like Tchouaméni, Liverpool doesn't look at other options that could still do a decent job. This typically leaves them short, so Liverpool's transfer strategy needs to be looked at and improved, especially now that we are no longer at the top.

Liverpool had a genuine interest in signing Jude Bellingham, a player they had targeted for a while. However, the sequence of events surrounding their pursuit of midfield reinforcements, from missing out on Tchouaméni and opting to wait for Bellingham, only to find themselves unable to compete for his signature due to financial constraints and not wanting to be involved in a bidding war, is undeniably perplexing and detrimental to both Liverpool's public image and squad re-development. Liverpool's decision-makers must learn from this, reassess their approach, and ensure better foresight for future transfers. We can't afford another season like the one we witnessed because we are waiting for the perfect fit.

After the match, Chris Pajak of Redmen TV expressed a concern that Liverpool's chances of securing a top-four finish could be in jeopardy without proper investment in the midfield during the January transfer window. Now we know with the fullness of time, Liverpool didn't add any midfielders in January, and Chris' prediction came true, narrowly missing out on a top-four finish. Supporters knew, but Liverpool didn't act.

Ajax 0 - 3 Liverpool

UEFA Champions League (MatchDay 5)
Wednesday, 26th October 2022
Johan Cruyff Arena

Liverpool's objective was to secure at least a draw to advance to the last sixteen of the Champions League, and given the team's inconsistent form, supporters didn't know what to expect. Uncertainty surrounded which version of Liverpool would show up for the crucial match. Despite a shaky beginning, Liverpool managed to find their rhythm and confidently netted three goals at the Johan Cruyff Arena, clinching a comfortable victory.

Liverpool opted for a different formation, deploying a diamond midfield with Fabinho positioned at the base, Jordan Henderson and Harvey Elliott occupying the middle, and Roberto Firmino at the tip. This tactical adjustment aimed to prevent Darwin Núñez from being isolated on the left wing. To support this setup, Jordan Henderson and Andy Robertson provided cover in the left channel, allowing Núñez to operate more centrally. However, this unexpected change was not flawless. Fabinho, in particular, found himself with an extensive area to cover, often appearing isolated. Before Liverpool's breakthrough, Ajax exploited the gaps in midfield by bypassing Fabinho on multiple occasions.

The match followed a familiar pattern in many games this season, with Liverpool conceding a significant chance within the first few minutes. In this instance, the ball fortuitously fell to Ajax in the box after a deflection off Roberto Firmino. Brian Brobbey displayed good strength to hold off Virgil van Dijk and laid the ball off to Steven Berghuis, who took a touch before unleashing a shot that struck the outside of the post. Liverpool was lucky that Berghuis missed the opportunity, as it could have significantly altered the game's course.

Ajax continued to pose a threat in the match's first thirty to forty minutes. A moment of loose passing from Trent Alexander-Arnold resulted in Berghuis narrowly missing the target with a curled effort. However, former Southampton player Dušan Tadić had the most straightforward opportunity to score. Joe Gomez's attempted interception inadvertently deflected the ball into the path of Ajax winger Brobbey, who delivered a cross to Tadić at the back post. Alisson rushed out and made himself big, but Trent, positioned alongside Alisson, blocked Tadić's shot as it was directed towards the goal. Once again, Liverpool were fortunate to escape unscathed from the situation. They could have easily found themselves 2-0 down with a mountain to climb.

Liverpool began to find their rhythm towards the end of the first half, resulting in the opening goal. Jordan Henderson displayed incredible vision and technique as he executed a perfectly weighted pass with the outside of his boot, directing it towards Mohamed Salah. The ball bounced favourably for Salah, giving him the ideal opportunity to capitalise. The quality of Henderson's pass was such that if Thiago had executed it, it would have been hailed as a demonstration of his immense skill. The pass was described as having "instructions" guiding Salah on how to finish the chance. Henderson's calculated bouncing pass allowed Salah to deftly lift the ball over Ajax goalkeeper Remko Pasveer, securing a 1-0 lead for Liverpool. Although it came against the run of play, it was undeniably a superbly executed goal.

Liverpool had a golden opportunity to double their lead just before halftime. Andy Robertson delivered an exquisite pass to Roberto Firmino, who found himself in plenty of space. Showing his selflessness, Firmino made a precise pass to Darwin Núñez, who had an excellent chance to score. However, Núñez's strike, unfortunately, hit the post despite the goal gaping. There were no excuses for the missed opportunity, and Núñez was visibly frustrated with himself as the referee blew the halftime whistle shortly after.

Fortunately, Núñez redeemed himself in the second half. He attempted a cross that turned into a shot, forcing Ajax goalkeeper Pasveer to punch the ball out for a corner. Robertson stepped up to take the corner, delivering an out-swinging cross, and Núñez expertly headed it into the far post. His performance on the pitch was described as chaotic, both exhilarating and frustrating, as seen with his earlier missed opportunity and the well-taken header. Due to his unpredictable style, fans have labelled Núñez as a maverick and a box-office striker. The chaos he brings to the game will be welcomed if he scores goals.

Liverpool extended their lead to 3-0 shortly after. Trent delivered a precise pass to Salah, who had plenty of time and space to turn and play a through ball to Harvey Elliott. With great power and accuracy, Elliott unleashed a high shot that found the back of the net. This well-executed and direct goal effectively put the match out of reach early in the second half. From then on, Liverpool needed to maintain their professionalism, avoid unnecessary risks, and focus on seeing out the remainder of the game. Which they were able to do.

The treatment the travelling Kop received in Amsterdam was highly praised, and there was a lot of positive feedback. Fans were respected and managed appropriately, without trouble, intimidation, or a post-match lock-in for the away supporters. The good-natured behaviour displayed by both sets of fans contributed to a peaceful atmosphere. It is common for away fans to be held back as home fans leave the stadium in European games, but it was unnecessary. The praise for the away experience was widely shared on social media platforms by James Pearce of The Athletic, the Merseyside Police Twitter account, The Spirit of Shankly (TSOS) supporters union, and the away fans in attendance. TSOS even stated that this should serve as a blueprint for all future European away games, highlighting the exemplary standards set during this match.

Liverpool's qualification to the last sixteen of the Champions League was confirmed with this victory, which was undoubtedly a positive outcome. While winning the group was still mathematically possible, it would be challenging given the goal difference required against Napoli. However, the important thing is that Liverpool had secured a place in the competition's knockout stages, ensuring they had European football to return to after the World Cup break and into the new year. Despite the team's inconsistent form, qualifying for the knockout stages of the Champions League should be seen as a small victory. Little did we know then that a two-legged tie against Real Madrid in the round of sixteen awaited us.

Liverpool 1 - 2 Leeds United

Premier League
Saturday, 29th October 2022
Anfield

Halloween was forty-eight hours away, but Liverpool Football Club gave supporters an early horror show. The team's league form was woeful, and a cause for concern, and the results resemble those from the end of Brendan Rodgers' period or even the earlier Roy Hodgson era. Ironically, Roy Hodgson's results at Liverpool were identical to this season's after twelve league matches. Winning four, drawing four, and losing four.

After the final whistle, I mistakenly turned to Twitter to gauge the feelings among fans. It turned out to be a regrettable decision. I quickly realised that immersing myself in strangers' negative and impulsive opinions only increased my disappointment and misery. In hindsight, I advise others to avoid social media after a loss. Trust me, your mental well- is more important than seeing the negativity on social media after a disappointing result.

Jürgen Klopp was trending on Twitter after the loss to Leeds United. Fans of Liverpool and fans of rival clubs criticised the German manager for his 'Liverpool were unlucky' comments following this loss. In reality, Liverpool's performance was far from unlucky. They were poor, and, unsurprisingly, many people took to social media to voice their disagreement.

There were the usual reactionary 'Klopp Out' tweets from fans who struggle to handle a loss. It brought to mind a recent comment by Neil Fitzmaurice on the Poetry in Motion podcast for the Liverpool Echo. Neil expressed his preference for every member of the squad to depart before Klopp. It was his way of highlighting Klopp's irreplaceable value, a sentiment I share.

Jürgen Klopp has been instrumental in repairing, reviving, and reinvigorating Liverpool Football Club. The recent successes Liverpool has achieved can largely be attributed to his leadership. While he is not immune to criticism, it's essential to consider how long he can be expected to work miracles with a net spend comparable to that of EFL Championship teams.

As for whether Fenway Sports Group (FSG) is to blame, their self-sufficient model might be facing a level of scrutiny we haven't witnessed before. Should FSG consider investing more? Most definitely. Should they provide the best manager in the world with more resources to work with? Absolutely. This squad requires a significant overhaul. Some players should be moved on, while new additions are necessary. Implementing such changes is easier said than done, but it still needs to be done. Will FSG be willing to undertake a complete squad overhaul? Probably not. However, they surprised me when they met Mohamed Salah's wage demands, despite my initial belief that they wouldn't compromise their wage structure for a single player. I hope to be proven wrong. Is it a matter of simply pouring money into the problem until it's resolved? That approach has worked wonders for Newcastle United, who secured a top-four finish.

Liverpool's primary objective for this season was to secure at least a fourth-place finish in the Premier League. Falling short of this minimum requirement should be considered a disaster, a complete capitulation, and a significant setback for the club. It was assumed that finishing outside the top four would impact their ability to attract top-tier players and delay the rebuilding process needed to compete at the highest level. Let's hope players are attracted to the project and the prospect of working under Jürgen Klopp. Now we know Liverpool will be playing in the Europa League.

Disaster struck for Liverpool within the first five minutes of the match against Leeds. As a recurring issue for the team, Leeds targeted Liverpool's right channel to exploit its vulnerability. Unfortunately, in this instance, in an attempt to regain possession, Joe Gomez played a blind pass back to Alisson without realising that the Alisson had moved to a different position in anticipation of a backpass from Gomez. The misguided pass ended up across the six-yard box, resulting in an easy tap-in goal for Rodrigo Moreno. Adding to the frustration, Alisson slipped when he realised the ball was wayward and couldn't recover his position.

Liverpool faced another uphill battle to get back into the match, which arose due to their mistakes. However, they managed to level the score thanks to a great goal by Mohamed Salah. Andy Robertson delivered a perfectly floated cross. Salah executed a superb volley at the back post, finding the net in the fourteenth minute, just ten minutes after Leeds' opening goal. Instead of capitalising on this momentum and asserting control, Liverpool failed to stifle Leeds, allowing them to regain confidence and create more chances. This shift in momentum gave Leeds hope and encouragement, making the task even more challenging for Liverpool.

In the second half, Liverpool managed to create some scoring opportunities, with Darwin Núñez coming close to finding the back of the net. Leeds goalkeeper Illan Meslier made some excellent saves to deny Núñez's shots. In the first half, Meslier also made a crucial tackle on Núñez when a well-placed pass from Trent Alexander-Arnold put him in a one-on-one situation. Although the easiest option seemed to be lobbing the out-of-position Meslier, Núñez hesitated and attempted to dribble past the goalkeeper, ultimately failing to do so. Núñez should have been more clinical with his shooting chances. However, it's important to remember that Liverpool's defeat cannot be solely attributed to his performance. The team's overall fragility and vulnerabilities were the main factors that contributed to their loss.

In the closing stages of the second half, Liverpool's efforts to find a winning goal were thwarted by the impressive performance of Leeds goalkeeper Meslier, who made several crucial saves to deny Liverpool's attempts throughout the match. Following the match, Klopp stated that he would have been content with a draw against Leeds. This was probably because of the significance of avoiding another defeat, but Leeds had different plans and pushed for a positive result.

The sequence leading to Leeds' winning goal began with their forward Wilfried Gnonto managing to deliver a cross, despite the efforts of James Milner and Curtis Jones to block it. The ball reached Patrick Bamford in the penalty area, who had a stroke of luck as his heavy touch ended up floating towards Crysencio Summerville a short distance away. Summerville displayed quick footwork, taking three touches in rapid succession. The first touch allowed him to control the ball, the second moved it away from Thiago, who was attempting to make a tackle, and the third touch was a shot that beat Alisson, despite the Brazilian goalkeeper managing to get a slight touch on the ball. The match was effectively decided at this moment, with Leeds coming to Anfield and securing the victory.

Anfield, known as a fortress, had lost an element of its aura of intimidation. Visiting teams were no longer fearful of playing there. The once-feared reputation has diminished, and opponents relish the opportunity to face Liverpool, regardless of whether it's a home or away fixture. Teams have realised they can exploit Liverpool's vulnerabilities, create difficulties for them, and contribute to their ongoing struggles.

Furthermore, the atmosphere at Anfield had been lacklustre. Fans expressed their discontent through audible moans and groans. On one occasion, when Harvey Elliott lost the ball in his half, the crowd's reaction prompted Fabinho to turn towards the Kop and gesture, indicating a desire for more support for the players rather than criticism. The harmony between the players and supporters was becoming tense as supporters became increasingly impatient for Liverpool to reverse their fortunes and salvage their season.

Ben Johnson, the writer responsible for player ratings on The Anfield Wrap fan media channel, made an insightful observation regarding Harvey Elliott's efforts to motivate the crowd. Johnson pointed out that Elliott's constant attempts to rally the crowd had become annoying instead of energising the fans. Johnson proposed that Elliott focus on motivating his teammates, as they are the ones in need of a boost to revive their performance levels. Something I fully agreed with.

Regardless of form, losing to teams like Nottingham Forest and Leeds United, both of which were in the relegation zone when they played Liverpool, is hugely disappointing.

Liverpool's performances have been far from their usual standards, and these defeats were seen as significant setbacks. Liverpool had become an easy target for opposing teams, giving them opportunities and failing to capitalise on their goal-scoring chances.

November

2022

- Napoli (H) - 1st November - UCL - Page 156

- Tottenham (A) - 6th - November - EPL - Page 160

- Derby (H) - 9th November - EFL Cup - Page 167

- Southampton (H) - 12th November - EPL - Page 173

Liverpool 2 - 0 Napoli

UEFA Champions League (Matchday 6)
Tuesday, 1st November 2022
Anfield

It was a much-needed victory for Liverpool against Napoli at Anfield. Napoli came into the match in excellent form, but Liverpool managed to match their opponent and secure a crucial win. The result ended Napoli's impressive unbeaten streak and showcased Liverpool's ability to compete with one of the most in-form teams in Europe. This victory starkly contrasted the previous encounter between the two sides, where Liverpool suffered a humiliating defeat. It was a positive step forward for the team and a reminder of their capabilities on the European stage.

Liverpool reverted to their familiar 4-3-3 formation. Although Curtis Jones was deployed as a makeshift left-winger, Roberto Firmino played in the centre, and Mohamed Salah was in his usual position on the right wing. Liverpool looked and performed better because of the familiarity of this formation. After the match, Salah spoke to BT Sport, and he got asked about his positioning:

It's not my job. It's the gaffer's job. Any position makes me comfortable. I'm happy about it. I played that position (on the right) [for] five or six years. I have to say that's the best for me. But, the manager decides the tactics. As the player, you have to follow the leader.

Salah's acknowledgement highlights his preference for the right-wing position, and it is likely that other Liverpool players also feel more at ease in the familiar 4-3-3 formation. The team's comfort in this setup was evident as they played with cohesion and defensive solidity against Napoli. The match was a balanced and competitive contest, with neither team dominating or asserting complete control as the game progressed. However, the 4-3-3 formation allowed Liverpool to remain compact and effectively match Napoli in crucial areas.

Napoli believed they had scored in the fifty-third minute when Leo Skiri Østigård headed in from a set piece. Liverpool's high defensive line was tested and exposed, but VAR intervened to check for offside. Although the review took over three minutes, it ultimately ruled Østigård offside, disallowing the goal.

It was in the eighty-fifth minute when Liverpool broke the deadlock. Kostas Tsimikas delivered a corner, and Darwin Núñez's header forced a brilliant goal-line save from Napoli's goalkeeper, Alex Meret. Núñez initially thought his shot had crossed the line and celebrated prematurely. At the same time, Salah capitalised on the rebound from Meret's save and ensured the ball went over the line, securing the goal. Núñez's attempt didn't cross the line, so the goal was credited to Salah. This goal also saw Salah equal Steven Gerrard's European goalscoring record, with both players having forty-one goals.

Liverpool's second goal followed a similar pattern, with Tsimikas delivering another corner and Virgil van Dijk heading towards goal. Once again, Meret made an impressive save, but the ball remained loose and rolled perilously close to the goal line. Núñez, unable to resist the opportunity, thundered the ball into the back of the net. Initially, the linesman raised the flag to signal an offside decision, leading to Virgil's comical reaction of putting his head in his hands with a wry smile. However, VAR intervened to review the offside call, and the replay showed that Piotr Zieliński had played Núñez onside. The goal was rightfully awarded, and even Virgil could see the funny side of the situation. Finally, with the goal given, the referee blew the final whistle, ending the match.

Liverpool's victory against Napoli provided a much-needed boost of confidence. There was hope that Liverpool could remain undefeated in their next three matches. The upcoming away game against Tottenham would be the toughest challenge on paper, but overcoming them would build further confidence for the remaining two games against Derby County in the EFL Cup and Southampton in the Premier League.

The draw for the last sixteen of the Champions League was scheduled for Monday, 7th November, and Liverpool knew their fate when paired with familiar opponents Real Madrid. The match against Real Madrid would offer a chance for redemption after their victory over Liverpool in the Champions League Final several months earlier. Sadly, Real Madrid seemed to be Liverpool's kryptonite, so dreams of some sweet revenge were soon met with the reality of facing the fourteen-time champions over two legs.

Tottenham 1 - 2 Liverpool

Premier League
Sunday 6th November 2022
Tottenham Hotspur Stadium

Liverpool's victory over Tottenham Hotspur was necessary considering the potential thirteen-point gap that could have opened between the two clubs had Tottenham won. The anxiety of falling so far behind this early in the season would have made any hopes of recovery seem daunting. The performance wasn't the most impressive, but securing the three points prevented the gap from widening and kept Liverpool's slim aspirations of a top-four finish alive.

Liverpool's decision to revert to the 4-3-3 formation proved beneficial, as it provided them with an advantage because of the player's familiarity and understanding. Over the years, Jürgen Klopp's Liverpool team has thrived with this formation, and the players are well-versed in their roles and responsibilities. They know where to be, how to coordinate runs and when to press the ball, and more. It brings a level of cohesion and efficiency to their gameplay. While Klopp's experimentation with different formations during Liverpool's slump can be understood, it is clear that the 4-3-3 formation was still the go-to choice, as long as injuries and available players allowed. It offers a sense of stability and a foundation that Liverpool can build upon, and it would have been the formation *I* would have liked Liverpool to use until I saw the freshness that the inverted fullback set-up brought for Liverpool later in the season.

During the match, Gary Neville, providing co-commentary on Sky Sports, highlighted how Tottenham's 5-3-2 formation unintentionally played into Liverpool's strengths. Neville pointed out that Tottenham's midfield three struggled to provide suitable cover when Liverpool executed their trademark full-back to full-back cross-field passes. This allowed Liverpool to exploit the spaces on the wings, particularly in the first half when they quickly switched the ball. As a result, Liverpool's left-back Andy Robertson found plenty of room to advance up the field and deliver forward passes to Darwin Núñez, who was positioned as the left-winger from the start of the game. This tactical advantage for Liverpool played a significant role in their success during the match.

Liverpool began the match positively, capitalising on Tottenham's tendency to start games slowly. This observation was widely shared among pundits and journalists and even confirmed by Andy Robertson in his post-match interview. It appeared that Liverpool had considered Tottenham's slow starts while preparing for the game.

In addition to Tottenham's tendency to start matches slowly, it is worth noting that they have shown resilience and an ability to perform better in the later stages of games. They have displayed the ability to score late winners and turn the tide in their favour. Recognising this, Liverpool needed to position themselves firmly in the match's early stages, aiming to take advantage of Tottenham's slow start and secure a goal or two. This would allow Liverpool to assert control over the game and approach the second half according to their preferred tactics, including the option of defending deep if Tottenham applied increased pressure in the latter stages of the match.

If this match was scripted, it unfolded according to plan. Liverpool found the back of the net twice in the first half, establishing a favourable lead. However, Tottenham showcased increased danger in the second half, scoring a goal and creating a tense and nerve-wracking final twenty minutes for Liverpool.

In the eleventh minute, Mohamed Salah provided Liverpool with the opening goal. It was a well-executed play that started with Robertson delivering a low cross from the left wing into the box. Darwin Núñez showed reasonable control and passed the ball to Salah, who swiftly took a touch, turned, and unleashed a shot with his second touch. The accuracy and power behind Salah's strike left Tottenham goalkeeper Hugo Lloris rooted to the spot, as he recognised the quality and power of the shot had already beaten him.

Before Salah scored his second goal, Liverpool had to endure pressure from Tottenham as they tried to stage a comeback. However, Liverpool managed to maintain control and limit Tottenham's opportunities. The closest Tottenham came to scoring was when Ivan Perišić connected with a cross from Harry Kane, heading the cross towards goal. But Liverpool goalkeeper Alisson intervened with a fantastic save, making himself big, and luckily the ball hit his head to divert the shot onto the post, preventing a goal. It was a crucial moment in the game that showed Alisson's reflexes and shot-stopping ability.

Salah extended Liverpool's lead in the fortieth minute with a brilliant display of anticipation and skill. Alisson launched a long ball forward, and Eric Dier's attempted header back to his goalkeeper fell short. Sensing an opportunity, Salah read the situation perfectly and intercepted the backpass attempt. It was refreshing for Liverpool to capitalise on an opponent's mistake. Salah then showed his dribbling ability, taking a couple of touches as he advanced into the box. With composure and finesse, he delicately chipped the ball over the onrushing Lloris, finding the back of the net. It was a great goal that highlighted Salah's talent. His performance indicated that he was finding his form, and his goal tally of fourteen in all competitions so far was an impressive testament to his scoring ability.

As anticipated, Tottenham kept to the script and emerged in the second half determined to turn the tide. With nothing to lose, they opted for an all-out attacking strategy. The match's momentum shifted in their favour, as reflected by the attacking moment graph from sofascore.com, which showed Tottenham's dominance in the second half.

During their intense attacking phase, Tottenham pulled a goal back in the second half, instilling a renewed hope of salvaging something positive from the match. Harry Kane showed his clinical finishing by capitalising on a well-executed pass from Dejan Kulusevski. Despite Ibrahima Konaté marking Kane, the prolific striker found the back of the net with a skilful shot from a challenging angle, leaving Alisson with no chance to make a save. From Liverpool's perspective, there were no significant errors on their part; the goal was simply a testament to Kane's ability in front of goal.

Following Tottenham's goal, Liverpool's attacking efforts slowed as they opted for a more cautious approach, focusing on maintaining defensive solidity rather than seeking further opportunities to extend their lead. This resulted in a limited number of poorly executed counterattacks. While there was a potential risk of conceding another goal, the Liverpool players displayed professionalism. They effectively managed the game, strategically wasting time when necessary during stoppages to run down the clock. The advantage gained from their first-half lead enabled them to use a deep defensive stance, absorb Tottenham's pressure, and successfully see out the match. Overall, Liverpool executed their game plan well, achieving an impressive result away from home.

Liverpool's first-half display was some of the best football they had played all season. They controlled and executed their game plan effectively, earning a well-deserved lead. Although their second-half performance may have left room for improvement, it is vital to consider the context of the match. Holding the lead allowed Liverpool to adopt a more cautious approach, prioritising defensive stability. While Tottenham had opportunities to level the score, Liverpool's resolute defence and some fortunate misses ensured the opposition couldn't capitalise on those chances. Ultimately, the most crucial aspect was that Liverpool emerged as the victors; securing the three points was all that mattered.

The victories over Napoli and Tottenham provided a much-needed boost to Liverpool's confidence and morale. These wins against tough opponents showed the team's ability to compete at a high level. However, it was equally crucial for Liverpool to carry this momentum forward and deliver strong performances against teams they were expected to beat. Inconsistency in gaining victories against so-called "lesser" teams was ultimately the downfall for Liverpool this season. If Liverpool had approached these matches with the same focus and determination, they would have been able to secure a top-four position easily.

Liverpool 0 - 0 Derby County
(3-2 on pens)

EFL Cup Third Round
Wednesday, 9th November 2022
Anfield

In the third round of the EFL Cup, a heavily rotated Liverpool team managed to secure the victory. The match ended in a goalless draw after the regular ninety minutes, leading to a penalty shootout to determine the winner. I appreciated the decision by the EFL to skip extra time and proceed directly to penalties, as it prevented the game from dragging on without any goals being scored. Even if the match had gone into extra time, it seemed unlikely that Liverpool or Derby would have found the back of the net, given the nature of the game. It was one of those occasions where scoring proved to be a challenge.

Liverpool's performance in the match was relatively comfortable, particularly for the defence. The duo of Joe Gomez and Nat Phillips, both experienced centre-backs, effectively handled Derby's limited attacking threats. Throughout the ninety minutes, goalkeeper Caoimhín

Kelleher had little involvement but emerged as the hero during the penalty shootout. It was also great to see Calvin Ramsay being handed his first start for the Liverpool first team. He displayed confidence, assertiveness, and composure on and off the ball. Additionally, it was satisfying to witness Kostas Tsimikas being given some game time. The Greek Scouser performed well.

The midfield trio of Alex Oxlade-Chamberlain, Bobby Clark, and Stefan Bajčetić also had a reasonably comfortable outing. Oxlade-Chamberlain took on the role of the experienced player in the midfield, guiding his younger teammates who are in the early stages of their careers. It was a mixed night for Oxlade-Chamberlain, as he couldn't significantly impact the match with his experience and skill set. However, considering it was his first start in several months, it provided a valuable opportunity for him to shake off any rustiness from not playing regularly. Overall, he performed fine, and the other two midfielders beside him also held their own in the match.

The front three of Fábio Carvalho, Layton Stewart, and Melkamu Frauendorf had a relatively quiet game and could not make a significant impact. Being the most experienced among the three at just twenty years of age, Carvalho couldn't create many scoring opportunities. The front three had limited chances to score, and none of the front three had a clear-cut opportunity to find the back of the net. Nevertheless, Jürgen Klopp would have been pleased to have given them valuable minutes in the first team, allowing them to gain experience at Anfield in a competitive match.

The second-half substitutions of Roberto Firmino and Darwin Núñez didn't quite have the desired impact for Liverpool either. Both players struggled to make an influence on the match and couldn't find the back of the net. However, the introduction of Harvey Elliott boosted Liverpool's attacking creativity, although they still couldn't convert their chances into goals.

A notable substitution was the introduction of Ben Doak just after the seventieth minute, which offered Liverpool a more direct option in their attacking play. Doak impressed supporters with his fearless runs at Derby's defence, showing a willingness to take risks and create opportunities for his team. Post-match, Jürgen Klopp was asked about the sixteen-year-old Scot's first-team debut:

That's Ben. His instructions were easy. 'Do what you do all the time,' He's a really lively boy, a smart player, a good dribbler, fast, can use both legs. It's good. It was nice to watch, really nice to watch. Coming in and immediately making an impact. A lot of things are obviously natural to him, which is really helpful. [I'm] pretty sure his family was here tonight. I can remember when I saw them at the AXA when we signed the boy and how excited everybody was. Tonight is the next step. It's cool.

To add to the positive week for Doak and his family, he was offered his first professional contract at the club just five days after making his debut. This achievement highlighted his talent and potential, and the reward of a contract was a testament to his hard work.

The prospect of a penalty shootout became increasingly likely as the game progressed. Despite Liverpool's efforts, they could not find a breakthrough against Derby's resilient defensive line. Penalties are known to be a game of chance, and even with a few more experienced players on the pitch at the final whistle, success was not guaranteed. The outcome of a penalty shootout is often unpredictable and can swing either way, adding to the tension.

The decision to allocate the whole of the Anfield Road End to Derby County fans created an interesting atmosphere within the grounds, and it might have been a regret since the penalties were to be taken at that end of the ground. The responsibility of taking the first penalty fell on the shoulders of eighteen-year-old Stefan Bajčetić, who unfortunately missed. While Bajčetić should be praised for his bravery in stepping up, it was a lot of responsibility for a young player when more experienced options were available. Additionally, there were concerns about the positioning of Derby's goalkeeper, Joe Wildsmith, who appeared to be off his line when saving the penalty. It's possible that the choice to have Bajčetić take the first penalty was based on the idea that there might be less pressure on the initial kick, but some would have preferred a more seasoned player to take that first spot-kick.

Kelleher's performance in the shootout was heroic, as he made three crucial saves to secure Liverpool's victory and progression to the fourth round. He has proven himself a reliable goalkeeper and deserves more opportunities to showcase his ability. However, he faces tough competition from Alisson, regarded as one of the world's best. Given the circumstances, Kelleher would have likely continued to feature in EFL Cup, and FA Cup matches, providing him more game time. Unfortunately, because of Liverpool's poor season and lack of a cup run, Kelleher didn't get many more chances to shine.

Liverpool 3 - 1 Southampton

Premier League
Saturday, 12th November 2022
Anfield

Liverpool's win against Southampton marked their fourth consecutive victory, highlighting the positive momentum the team had built before the break for the World Cup. The timing of the break felt somewhat frustrating, especially considering the team's improved form. It was understandable to feel excitement for the upcoming World Cup and a longing for Liverpool's form to continue. While the break interrupted the club's momentum, it also allowed some players to rest, regroup, and prepare for the challenges ahead.

I had some concerns leading up to this match. The managerial change at Southampton and the potential impact of players representing their countries in the World Cup made me apprehensive. I feared a possible "new manager bounce" and was worried Liverpool players could hold back to avoid injuries. However, my worries were unfounded as

Liverpool handled the situation professionally and secured the victory.

Liverpool wasted no time breaking the deadlock, finding the back of the net early in the game. From a deep free-kick, Andy Robertson delivered a well-placed ball into the box. Roberto Firmino rose above the defenders and executed a powerful header from sixteen yards out, sending the ball curling into the far corner of the net. Southampton goalkeeper Gavin Bazunu's positioning was poor, contributing to the goal. While Firmino may have intended to direct the ball towards the back post for a teammate, his execution resulted in a goal for himself.

Unfortunately, Firmino's omission from the Brazil World Cup squad came as a disappointment for both him and Liverpool fans. Jürgen Klopp expressed that Firmino was undoubtedly affected by the news. The statistics show Firmino's numbers stacked up favourably against other Brazilian attackers. Firmino has been a significant contributor for Liverpool in the early stages of this season, with twelve goal contributions comprising eight goals and four assists. Comparatively, players like Richarlison, Antony, Gabriel Martinelli, and Raphinha recorded fewer goal contributions. Understandably, fans would argue there was a place for

Firmino in the national squad based on his performances and productivity.

Southampton's quick equaliser in the ninth minute came from a well-executed set piece. James Ward-Prowse, known for his ability in dead ball situations, delivered a perfectly lofted ball into the box. Ché Adams made an excellently timed run, evading Virgil van Dijk, and headed the ball into the net to level the score. Despite conceding, Liverpool remained in control and continued to perform well. Alisson, visibly disappointed, reacted by holding his head in his hands, hoping to maintain a clean sheet to match his new clean-shaven appearance.

Darwin Núñez showcased his full range of skills and had an outstanding performance that could be considered his best in a Liverpool shirt. He constantly threatened Southampton's defence, causing them all sorts of problems. Núñez was pivotal in Liverpool's victory and contributed two crucial goals in the first half. His opening goal was a display of composure and technique. Harvey Elliott delivered a well-executed chipped-through pass from outside the box, finding Núñez, who calmly volleyed the ball with the inside of his foot, showing coolness in front of the goal. It was an impressive finish from the striker.

In the build-up to Núñez's second goal, Liverpool showed their quick and precise attacking play. A short set piece enabled Liverpool to transition into an attacking area swiftly. Thiago initiated the move with a simple ten-yard pass to Firmino, who had plenty of time and space. Using his vision, Firmino delivered a perfectly weighted through ball that split Southampton's right back and right winger, who was tracking back defensively. Capitalising on Firmino's pass, Andy Robertson instinctively drove the ball low across the box with his first touch. Núñez reacted quickly, sliding in to connect with the ball and find the back of the net. It was a sleek display of football from Liverpool, allowing them to enter halftime with a commanding 3-1 lead.

Alisson's outstanding performance in the second half proved crucial, as he made several vital saves to keep Liverpool ahead. He displayed his shot-stopping abilities with a crucial left-hand save to deny a Mohamed Elyounoussi shot. Alisson also showed his bravery and quick reactions by rushing out to smother a one-on-one chance from Samuel Edozie, making himself big and preventing a Southampton goal. Furthermore, he displayed agility and athleticism with a diving save to his right to deny a Ché Adams header. All three saves were instrumental in preserving Liverpool's lead and securing the three points. Alisson, not for the first time throughout the season, was immense.

Heading into the break for the World Cup, Liverpool's position of sixth in the Premier League, seven points behind fourth-placed Tottenham (with a game in hand), was certainly different from where many expected the team to be at the start of the season. It had been a challenging and unexpected journey, forcing fans, including myself, to readjust our expectations. While improvements were needed, Liverpool still had a chance to achieve their target of securing a top-four finish. However, inconsistent form meant Liverpool made it more difficult for themselves.

December

2022

- Man City (A) - 22nd December - EFL Cup - Page 180

- Aston Villa (A) - 26th December - EPL - Page 188

- Leicester (H) - 30th December - EPL - Page 193

Manchester City 3 - 2 Liverpool

EFL Cup 4th Round
Thursday, 22nd December 2022
Etihad Stadium

Liverpool's return to action after the World Cup resulted in a disappointing defeat in the EFL Cup. The nature of the competition allowed squad rotation and players to regain match fitness and lose rustiness. However, Liverpool had to contend with the absence of key players. Virgil van Dijk, Alisson Becker, and Ibrahima Konaté were not included in the matchday squad due to the extended rest after their involvement in the later stages of the World Cup. Trent Alexander-Arnold was unavailable due to illness, while Roberto Firmino was sidelined with a calf injury.

The optimism surrounding Liverpool's second half of the season took a hit when Luis Díaz and Diogo Jota suffered setbacks in their recoveries from injury. Both players were expected to contribute significantly to the team upon their return, but unfortunately, things didn't go as planned. Díaz had been out with a knee injury and had to undergo surgery, further delaying his return. As for Jota, the Liverpool medical staff remained hopeful that he would return in the new year, indicating that his recovery had encountered some challenges.

Matches against Manchester City, especially away from home, are always challenging and highly competitive. The rivalry between the two teams always adds extra intensity and desire to secure victory. Whether it's a Premier League encounter, a cup fixture, or any other competition, Liverpool and Manchester City have strong ambitions to be the team that comes out on top. Losing these matches is disappointing, considering the high stakes and the desire to assert dominance over a fierce rival.

Manchester City's aggressive pressing style can be challenging to contend with, and they certainly made their presence felt in the match's opening stages. Liverpool tried to remain composed and stuck to their game plan of playing out from the back. While they could successfully bypass City's press on a few occasions, there were instances where the pressure forced Liverpool into making risky passes into midfield, leading to turnovers in dangerous areas of the pitch. Coping with City's pressing requires a combination of careful decision-making, precise passing, and quick movement on and off the ball. Liverpool faced challenges in executing these aspects consistently during the early exchanges of the match.

In the tenth minute, Manchester City's aggressive approach yielded results as they managed to break the deadlock. Kevin De Bruyne and Erling Haaland combined effectively to create the goal-scoring opportunity. De Bruyne delivered a precise cross from the left flank, while Haaland displayed his clinical finishing ability by sidefoot-volleying the ball past Liverpool's goalkeeper, Caoimhín Kelleher. Upon reflection, it can be said that the defending from Joe Gomez could have been better, as he allowed Haaland to find space in front of him. Still, credit must be given to Manchester City for their deserving lead, capitalising on the chance from their talented duo.

As the match progressed, Liverpool's struggle to cope with Manchester City's aggressive approach raised concerns among supporters, including myself. City's midfield trio of Rodri, İlkay Gündoğan, and Kevin De Bruyne demonstrated their dominance, outplaying Liverpool's midfield consisting of Thiago, Harvey Elliott, and Stefan Bajčetić. On paper, it is clear that those three City midfielders would dominate against Liverpool's midfield three. However, despite the difficulties, Liverpool found an equaliser just ten minutes after City's opening goal, and it came with their first shot on target. The goal provided a moment of relief and hope for Liverpool, showing their resilience and ability to make an impact even when faced with difficulties.

The equalising goal for Liverpool was a well-worked team effort. Joël Matip's forward dribble created space and allowed him to pass to James Milner, who drew several City players out of position. Milner showed composure inside the box and found Fábio Carvalho, who calmly placed the ball into the far corner of the net. It was a well-taken goal by Carvalho. However, it should be acknowledged that Carvalho, playing in an unfamiliar position as the left-sided forward, had a mixed performance overall. Judging him based on this away game against a challenging opponent like Manchester City would be unfair. Despite the goal, Carvalho struggled and seemed somewhat out of his depth, which is understandable considering the circumstances and the opposition.

Carvalho was substituted at halftime, and it is unknown whether this was a pre-match decision or a substitution based on his performance. His replacement was Alex Oxlade-Chamberlain. Stefan Bajčetić was also substituted at halftime for Fabinho. Bajčetić had a difficult night, dealing with the much more experienced midfield three against him. Again, he is still growing and learning in this Liverpool side, but the manager's faith in the player must have given him plenty of confidence. James Milner had to go off after thirty-eight minutes due to injury. Milner, playing right-back against the energetic and dangerous Cole Palmer, was substituted after feeling pain in his hamstring, and the decision was not to risk continuing. He was replaced by Nat Phillips, meaning Joe Gomez was switched to the right-back position. At the start of the second half, Liverpool had already made three substitutions, and it was 1-1.

Manchester City's second goal resulted from a misplaced pass by Thiago in midfield, which led to the ball reaching Rodri in a dangerous position. Rodri played a through ball to Riyad Mahrez, positioned inside the box. Mahrez demonstrated exceptional control with his first touch, evading the challenge of Andrew Robertson, and calmly finished the ball into the far corner of the net. It was a well-executed goal from Mahrez, and from Liverpool's perspective, it wasn't easy to defend. There was little Robertson, or any other defender, could have done to prevent the goal, given Mahrez's skill and precision.

Liverpool found their second equaliser through a swift and direct attack utilising Darwin Núñez's pace. Alex Oxlade-

Chamberlain played a perfectly-weighted outside-of-the-boot pass down the left wing, allowing Núñez to sprint onto it. Núñez used his speed to outpace Aymeric Laporte and deliver a pass to Mohamed Salah, who was positioned centrally in the box. It appeared that Salah wasn't initially anticipating the pass, but he quickly adjusted his position and skillfully sidefooted the ball into the back of the empty net. Ederson, Manchester City's goalkeeper, had come off his line to close down Núñez, leaving his goal exposed and making Salah's finish appear straightforward. It was a well-executed team goal to equalise for the second time.

Liverpool's hopes of salvaging a result suffered another setback as they conceded their third goal, ultimately proving to be the match-winner for Manchester City. The frustrating aspect of this goal was that it could have been prevented with better concentration from Liverpool. Manchester City opted for a short corner, with Kevin De Bruyne quickly taking it and exchanging passes with Palmer. De Bruyne then delivered a dangerous cross into the box, where Nathan Aké rose to head the ball into the net. Jordan Henderson was the only Liverpool player alert to the situation, but his efforts alone couldn't prevent the goal. A disappointing lapse in concentration from Liverpool allowed them to be caught out by City's swift and well-executed set piece.

After the match, there were criticisms directed at Darwin Núñez for his missed opportunities. He had several good chances where he dragged the ball wide and failed to hit the target with any of his shots, which was disappointing. The criticism towards him is understandable, as missed opportunities can significantly impact the game's outcome, but it wasn't pleasant to see. Joe Gomez also faced criticism for his performance, particularly with Erling Haaland's goal that opened the scoring. However, when Gomez was shifted to right-back to cover for the substitution of James Milner, his performance improved slightly. On a positive note, Nat Phillips received praise for his contributions after coming on as a substitute. He made some crucial blocks to deny City's dangerous shots and notably tackled Haaland during a one-on-one situation. Phillips impressed supporters with his defensive abilities and demonstrated a solid performance on the pitch.

There was room for improvement, but losing a fourth-round EFL Cup tie against Manchester City was not the end of the world for Liverpool. The upcoming Boxing Day match against Aston Villa was where the real test lied and held even greater importance because of Liverpool's poor position in the league.

Aston Villa 1 - 3 Liverpool

Premier League
Monday, 26th December 2022
Villa Park

Liverpool's victory against Aston Villa on Boxing Day was a hard-fought one. Despite facing challenges, Liverpool managed to secure the three points. The return of Virgil van Dijk to the central defence provided a boost, while Alex Oxlade-Chamberlain was given a starting opportunity. The match wasn't comfortable for Liverpool, but they displayed resilience to come out on top. It was a good win against a good team which showed Liverpool's ability to grind out results when needed.

Liverpool's opening goal against Aston Villa came from a set-piece shortly after a collision at the back involving Tyrone Mings and goalkeeper Robin Olsen. Andy Robertson took the corner, which was initially cleared. Trent Alexander-Arnold showed his vision with a remarkable outside-of-the-boot pass back to find Robertson, who made a well-timed run, still on the right wing from taking the corner. Robertson's intelligent positioning allowed him to meet Trent's pass perfectly, and he wasted no time delivering a first-time cross into the box. Per his poacher's instinct, Mohamed Salah anticipated the cross and positioned himself perfectly to receive the ball. With composure and precision, Salah calmly slotted the ball into the net, leaving the Villa goalkeeper with no chance of making a save. The goal highlighted the understanding between Liverpool's fullbacks and solidified Robertson's position as the top assist provider for defenders. Robertson had now surpassed the previous record held by Leighton Baines of Everton.

Liverpool's vulnerability in defence was seen again as Aston Villa created several promising opportunities to level the scoreline. Ollie Watkins, in particular, had multiple chances that he would have expected to convert into goals, while Leon Bailey squandered a clear opportunity to test the Liverpool goalkeeper. The match was back-and-forth, with both teams trading attacking moves and creating chances. The end-to-end action kept the supporters on the edge of their seats. Still, Liverpool could count themselves fortunate that Aston Villa failed to capitalise on their opportunities to draw level.

Liverpool's persistence in attack paid off as they extended their lead through a well-worked goal. Trent Alexander-

Arnold's corner caused chaos in the Aston Villa box, leading to a scramble for possession. Amid the chaos, Mohamed Salah displayed strength and composure, holding off the Villa defenders and finding Virgil van Dijk in a dangerous position. Virgil unleashed a powerful half-volley into the bottom corner, leaving the goalkeeper no chance.

Aston Villa's Ollie Watkins eventually made his mark on the match by pulling a goal back for his team during the second half. After having a goal disallowed for offside earlier, Watkins redeemed himself with a well-executed header from Douglas Luiz's precise delivery to the back post. His goal injected renewed hope and energy into Villa's performance, narrowing the deficit and putting pressure on Liverpool.

The third goal in any match often carries significant importance. It can solidify a team's lead, put them almost out of reach, or ignite a comeback spirit within the trailing side. For Liverpool, it was crucial to prevent Villa from scoring another goal and gaining further momentum. They needed to maintain their defensive discipline and resilience to win the match and secure the three points.

Thankfully, Stefan Bajčetić found the back of the net to restore Liverpool's two-goal lead. The sequence leading up to the goal showed Núñez's determination, as he managed to keep the ball in play and deliver it into a dangerous area. Aston Villa goalkeeper Robin Olsen was forced to react quickly, palming the ball away from the goal, but it fell into a central position in the box. Bajčetić demonstrated great composure and awareness as he calmly touched the ball over the rushing Olsen. With Tyrone Mings positioned on the goal line to cover, Bajčetić cleverly placed his shot through Mings' legs and into the net. It was a well-taken goal, highlighting the young player's talent and potential. The significance of this moment was clear in Bajčetić's post-match comments on Instagram, where he expressed that scoring the goal was the best moment of his life. It was a heartwarming moment for the young lad, and his teammates and fans alike shared in his joy and celebration.

Stefan Bajčetić's emergence as a surprise package this season has undoubtedly been a positive development for Liverpool. Coming into the first team during a challenging period for the club, Bajčetić displayed a fearlessness and energy that injected new life into Liverpool's midfield. One of the crucial aspects of Bajčetić's contributions was his versatility. He showcased his abilities in the defensive midfield role, playing as the number six and in the more attacking role as the number eight. Regardless of the position he was deployed in, Bajčetić impressed with his performances. At such a young age, Bajčetić has already demonstrated bags of potential, an exciting prospect for supporters. His impact on the team during crucial moments indicated that he has a promising future ahead of him.

After the match, rumours about Liverpool's interest in PSV Eindhoven player Cody Gakpo were circulating. Speculation grew when reliable journalist Paul Joyce from The Times tweeted about advanced talks between the two clubs. Soon after, the official PSV Eindhoven Twitter account confirmed that a deal had been agreed with Liverpool for Gakpo. It was an exciting addition to Liverpool's squad and a welcome late Christmas present for the fans. Despite Liverpool crying out for midfielders, the arrival of Gakpo made more sense every time we saw him play. He seamlessly learnt the role of Liverpool's false nine position and contributed big moments in the second half of the season.

Liverpool 2 - 1 Leicester City

Premier League
Friday, 30th December 2022
Anfield

Sometimes luck can play a huge role in a match, and while Liverpool may have been fortunate to come away with a win, it's important to acknowledge where they need improvement. The game at Anfield highlighted some issues, including a lack of cutting-edge in their attack and vulnerability at the back. The pressing play, a trademark of Liverpool's style, appeared lacklustre and disjointed. Instead of pressing as a cohesive unit, they engaged in individual pressing, which left gaps for the opposition to exploit. It's clear that for their pressing strategy to be successful, it requires collective effort and coordination. This match served as a reminder for Liverpool to address these shortcomings.

The early goal conceded against Leicester *again* highlighted Liverpool's ongoing defensive struggles. Seeing this pattern repeat itself was concerning, as it suggested a deeper issue. While the midfield's role in providing defensive protection is crucial, the defenders must also take responsibility for their performances. To address this problem, Liverpool needed to focus on improving defensive organisation and positioning as a collective unit. This required better communication and coordination between the midfield and defence to ensure adequate coverage to prevent early goals. The defenders needed to be more alert, focused, and proactive in their actions, including timely tackles and interceptions. Conceding the first goal, sometimes early in the match, was one of the most significant issues that needed addressing.

Leicester's goal resulted from a series of defensive errors and miscommunication from Liverpool. The breakdown in defence began with an unsuccessful challenge from Jordan Henderson, allowing Kiernan Dewsbury-Hall to evade the tackle and progress forward. Liverpool's defensive shape was compromised at this crucial moment, leaving them vulnerable. Andy Robertson's indecision regarding the offside trap further exposed Liverpool's defensive fragility. Unfortunately, his decision to play the trap and catch Ayoze Pérez offside proved the wrong choice. Dewsbury-Hall opted *not* to pass to Pérez and exploited the open space in Liverpool's defence. This lack of coordination and poor decision-making allowed Dewsbury-Hall to breach the backline and convert the chance past Alisson.

Falling behind early in matches puts additional pressure on the team and boosts the opposition's confidence. It disrupts Liverpool's game plan and requires more effort to mount a comeback. It was exhausting, and the stats proved the issue. Liverpool played fifty-two matches in the 2022/23 season, conceding the first goal in twenty-one games, which amounted to 40.38%. It simply hadn't been good enough.

Despite Liverpool's below-par performance, they managed to turn the game around thanks to two bizarre own goals from Leicester defender Wout Faes. The first own goal was a stroke of misfortune for Faes. Trent Alexander-Arnold delivered a low cross into the box, but none of Liverpool's players made a decisive attempt to attack it. Faes went for a slide tackle to clear the danger but inadvertently deflected the ball off the top of his foot. The deflection looped over Danny Ward and into the goal off the post. Faes couldn't replicate it even if he tried. During the halftime analysis and replays, it became evident that Ward had called for Faes to leave the cross, signalling that he could collect the ball easily. There was clear communication from Ward, but Faes either disregarded his goalkeeper's instruction or failed to hear it amidst the chaos in the box.

Faes became the unintentional villain for Leicester as he scored a second own goal. If the first resulted from misfortune, the second could only be described as a moment of foolishness. As Darwin Núñez made a run towards the goal, he cleverly chipped the ball over the onrushing Danny Ward, who was trying to make it difficult for Núñez to score. With no Liverpool players nearby, Núñez's delicate chip struck the post. In a bewildering moment, Faes inadvertently directed the ball into the back of his net while attempting to clear it. Upon reviewing the replay, it appeared peculiar, almost as if Faes intentionally buried the ball into the net after it hit the post. A baffling sequence of events ultimately sealed Liverpool's comeback, and the score remained unchanged until the final whistle.

While winning is always the aim, it was understandable to be concerned about Liverpool's poor performance against Leicester City. Virgil Van Dijk's post-match acknowledgement of the need for improvement and Trent Alexander-Arnold's perspective of moving forward with the points are both valid. However, It's important for Liverpool to not solely rely on luck and recognise that consistent, quality performances are necessary to achieve their goals. Liverpool *must* strive for better performances to ensure their success in the long run. The problem with luck is that it runs out.

January

2023

■ Brentford (A) - 2nd January - EPL - Page 200

■ Wolves (H) - 7th January - FA Cup - Page 206

■ Brighton (A) - 14th January - EPL - Page 213

■ Wolves (A) - 17th January - FAC Replay - Page 220

■ Chelsea (H) - 21st January - EPL - Page 224

■ Brighton (A) - 29th January - FA Cup - Page 228

Brentford 3 - 1 Liverpool

Premier League
Monday, 2nd January 2023
Gtech Community Stadium

Liverpool's performance against Brentford was far from their best, and seeing the team struggling to find their rhythm after the World Cup was tough. The first half was particularly lacklustre, and it's clear that the team's intensity and identity were missing. Jim Beglin's observation of Brentford's superior work ethic compared to Liverpool's was valid. Liverpool has a talented squad, but their work ethic and cohesion on the field have faltered. Brentford worked harder, which made it seem they wanted the three points more. At the turn of the year, Liverpool needed to reflect, regroup, and reignite their winning mentality to get back on track. Otherwise, it would be a very difficult second half of the season.

It was disheartening to see Liverpool lacking the passion and intensity that have been synonymous with Jürgen Klopp's teams. The team's performances were far from the standard we expected. Every team goes through cycles, and perhaps Liverpool was experiencing the end of their successful period. Football is a dynamic sport, and teams go through ups and downs. This was undoubtedly a challenging phase for Liverpool and its supporters. It was 2nd January, and fans were already looking to the season's end in May for a break.

Opta's statistics highlighted another concerning trend. Liverpool conceded many chances compared to the teams above them in the Premier League. This defensive fragility had contributed to dropping more points this season than in the previous campaign, and it was only January. The comparison with last season's performance was a stark reminder of Liverpool's challenges. With the season ongoing, Liverpool had an opportunity to rectify their shortcomings, but it felt unrealistic.

The first half of the match was undoubtedly a struggle for Liverpool, with Brentford having several close chances. Although two goals were rightly ruled offside, Brentford continued to cause problems and eventually scored from a corner. Ibrahima Konaté was unfortunate as the ball deflected off his shin, and, despite Alisson's efforts, it crossed the line. It was an unlucky moment for Konaté and Liverpool, which resulted in Brentford taking a 1-0 lead.

In a series of idiotic events, Liverpool conceded another goal just before halftime. Following *another* disallowed goal for Brentford due to offside, Alisson quickly distributed the ball from a free kick into midfield. However, Harvey Elliott unexpectedly dummied the ball without communicating with his teammates, resulting in Brentford regaining possession. Elliott couldn't have had a shout to leave it from another player in red because there were no Liverpool players around him.

Brentford regained possession from Elliott's dummy, and moments later, the ball found its way to Yoane Wissa at the back post. Wissa's header, which initially looked like Alisson saved, was unfortunately over the line. The goal-line technology confirmed that the ball had crossed the line, which extended Brentford's lead to 2-0 at halftime. It was a frustrating and avoidable goal to concede after escaping from the original disallowed goal.

In the second half, Jürgen Klopp made three halftime substitutions to try and turn the game around. Naby Keïta replaced Harvey Elliott, Kostas Tsimikas made way for Andy Robertson and Virgil van Dijk was substituted due to a hamstring issue, with Ibrahima Konaté taking his place. Klopp later confirmed that he didn't want to take any risks with Virgil's injury.

Liverpool showed improvement in their performance during the second half. They showed more enthusiasm and determination, raising questions about why they didn't show the same energy and desire in the first half. It was frustrating to see Liverpool's reactive nature, where they perform better after falling behind a goal or two. The team needed to start matches with the same level of determination they showed when chasing a deficit to assert their dominance from the beginning.

Liverpool's goal provided a glimmer of hope for a potential comeback. Trent Alexander-Arnold's excellent left-footed cross into the box found Alex Oxlade-Chamberlain, who timed his header perfectly to guide the ball into the net.

Following the goal, Liverpool seemed rejuvenated and determined to turn the tide in their favour. They began to gain control, with Brentford retreating and expecting further pressure from the Reds. Liverpool's increased control and presence in dangerous areas gave the impression that they could complete the comeback and secure a positive result.

However, In the match's dying moments, Liverpool's hopes of a comeback were shattered when Brentford sealed the victory with a late third goal. It was another frustrating moment for Liverpool as Ibrahima Konaté was dispossessed too easily by Bryan Mbeumo. Despite Mbeumo giving Konaté a slight nudge during their battle for the ball, the contact wasn't deemed enough to be considered a foul. Considering Konaté's physical attributes and defensive capabilities, it was particularly frustrating to witness him being outmuscled. Mbeumo capitalised on winning possession and calmly slotted the ball into the net, securing Brentford's 3-1 triumph.

The situation Liverpool found themselves in was undeniably challenging. While a midfield signing could have addressed some of their issues, Liverpool made no further additions. Considering the team's need for reinforcements in midfield, this decision raised concerns about their lack of ability to address their problems until at least the summer window, which meant risking the chance of missing out on a top-four spot.

Although the arrival of Cody Gakpo was a positive move, some questioned prioritising him over a midfielder, especially considering Liverpool's desperation for midfielders. The team's hopes of securing a top-four finish were increasingly at risk with every dropped point, and disappointing results like the one against Brentford undoubtedly affected team confidence.

Jamie Carragher summed things up perfectly during his post-match analysis for Sky Sports. Carragher went on a rant aimed at the club and the current state of affairs:

Liverpool has had problems all season against teams who are physical. When the game has intensity, they can't cope. This is a team, let's not forget, that pride itself on saying intensity is our identity. They can't cope with that anymore at this moment. It looks like an ageing team coming to an end, and that [Brentford match] was absolutely shambolic first half. Liverpool's transfer committee and Jürgen Klopp have been lauded more than any scouting network worldwide. This is on them. One midfield player signed in four-and-a-half years. They are running on fumes.

The team needed to find ways to address their issues, whether through tactical adjustments, improved performances from existing players, or a collective belief in their abilities. The road ahead was challenging, but Liverpool's eventual change to the inverted fullback formation showed reasons to be optimistic for the future.

Liverpool 2 - 2 Wolves

FA Cup Third-Round
Saturday, 7th January 2023
Anfield

Liverpool's draw with Wolves in the FA Cup third round only added to the mounting challenges. Because of the draw, there would be a replay to determine the winner, and the prospect of an additional match was far from ideal. The performance against Wolves was another disappointment, characterised by a lacklustre and below-par performance. The pattern of conceding first, attempting a comeback, conceding again, and struggling to break down organised defensive opponents had become all too familiar. It felt as though the team was stuck in a cycle that was difficult to break, and the supporters were feeling exhausted.

Liverpool's decision to field their strongest possible lineup in the FA Cup match against Wolves indicated their intention to take the competition seriously. Despite the opportunity for rotation, Jürgen Klopp opted to field a lineup consisting of predominantly first-team players. While some fans may have expected rotation and the inclusion of fringe players such as

Caoimhín Kelleher, Nat Phillips, or Stefan Bajčetić, Klopp's decision to go with a strong lineup showed their intention to perform well in the tournament.

Liverpool showed early dominance in the match, maintaining control and applying pressure on Wolves. Their high intensity and ball control troubled the Wolves' defence, creating opportunities to score. However, despite their positive start, Liverpool failed to convert their early dominance into goals. Football is a dynamic game, and the tide can quickly turn, so the team needed to stay focused in their pursuit of goals. Without goals, Liverpool's dominance was all for nothing.

Jürgen Klopp's decision to start the first team to secure a victory and create confidence was understandable. The fear of losing and prolonging the misery can drive a manager to field a strong lineup. However, the strategy did not have the desired outcome in this instance. Despite fielding the first team and making a strong start, Liverpool delivered a disappointing performance, which may have further dented their confidence rather than boosted it.

The season of goodwill and gift-giving ended two weeks earlier. That is unless you played in defence for Liverpool, who continued to give away gifts on a match-by-match basis.

Joël Matip and Alisson made costly errors, gifting Wolverhampton a goal–Matip's momentary lapse while in possession in the box was fortunate to go unpunished. However, the real blow came when Alisson made a glaring mistake. His attempted pass to Trent Alexander-Arnold was intercepted by Gonçalo Guedes, who capitalised on the gifted opportunity and scored into an open net.

Alisson was responsible for the error that directly led to Wolves taking the lead. However, it's worth acknowledging that Alisson has been instrumental for the team numerous times, and mistakes will always occur when goalkeepers are tasked with playing with their feet. Furthermore, if anybody has credit in the bank to allow for a mistake, it was Alisson.

Despite the break for the World Cup, which offered a chance to regroup and reassess, little had changed. Even with a mini Dubai break allowing non-World Cup participants to train in warmer weather, the team's performance remained stagnant. The underlying causes of Liverpool's decline included injuries to crucial players, defensive vulnerabilities, inconsistencies in form, and the potential fatigue from the previous season. These factors combined have contributed to the team's struggles. It all became so overwhelming and inescapable.

To add to the frustrations, Liverpool made no signings in the midfield during the January transfer window. The glaring issue in Liverpool's midfield has been clear to everyone, including Jürgen Klopp, who acknowledged it earlier in the season. The need for new midfielders was not an overreaction but a clear necessity. The club's failure to conduct business for a midfielder showed a concerning disregard for the team's needs, and this neglect had repercussions. Jamie Carragher summarised the situation after the Brentford match perfectly. One midfield signing in four and a half years is unacceptable for a club like Liverpool.

One joyous moment to highlight from the match was Darwin Núñez's equalising goal. The opportunity arose when Wolves defender Nathan Collins lost possession while attempting to switch the ball from one wing to another. Seizing the chance, Trent Alexander-Arnold, positioned on the right wing, collected the loose ball and swiftly advanced. With great vision, Trent delivered an impeccably accurate long pass to Núñez, who had positioned himself on the shoulder of the last defender. The pass was so precise that Núñez didn't need to alter his direction or speed. Showing excellent technique, he connected perfectly with the ball and skillfully guided it into the bottom corner of the net. It was a stunning goal, providing a much-needed boost for Liverpool and putting them back in the game.

In the fifty-second minute, Mohamed Salah scored a goal that gave Liverpool the lead. However, the goal was surrounded by controversy due to an offside decision. Cody Gakpo played a chipped pass forward into the box for Salah, who appeared to be offside. Wolves defender Toti Gomes attempted to clear the ball with a header, but his clearance went awry, causing it to flick deeper into the box, where Salah collected it, turned, and calmly side-footed it into the goal. The controversy arose from the interpretation of the offside rule. If Toti had not made contact with the ball, Salah would have been offside, and the goal would not have counted. However, because Toti made an attempt to play the ball and was unlucky with his clearance, the offside decision was overturned, and the goal was allowed to stand.

While the goal benefited Liverpool, it raised questions about the current offside rule and how defenders can be penalised for attempting to clear the ball and do their job. Some argue that these rules should be reviewed to avoid punishing defenders for their defensive instincts and actions.

Nevertheless, Liverpool had taken the lead at that moment, but the controversy was far from over.

Wolves managed to equalise in the game, bringing the scoreline to 2-2. The goal came as a result of a well-executed attacking move. Substitute Hwang Hee-chan, who had been on the pitch for only three minutes, combined with Matheus Cunha in a quick one-two pass sequence inside Liverpool's box. Unfortunately, Jordan Henderson failed to track Hwang's movement, allowing him to receive the return pass. The ball deflected off Ibrahima Konaté, who had attempted to come across and cover the danger. Unfortunately for Liverpool, the deflected ball struck Hwang and went underneath Alisson for an unexpected but deserved equaliser.

Following Wolves' equaliser, the match was filled with controversy once again. A corner from Matheus Nunes was initially cleared by Liverpool, only to be returned into the box by the corner taker, Nunes. Thiago attempted to clear the ball, but his clearance was poor, leading to a loose ball dropping for Hwang. Hwang then passed the ball to Toti, who skillfully backheeled it into the net, resulting in wild celebrations from the Wolves players, who believed they had secured a late victory.

However, their celebrations were cut short by the linesman's offside flag. The situation was then referred to VAR, which operated at Anfield but not at all the grounds for the other third-round fixtures, which always irritates me. Have VAR at every ground, or don't use it. Unfortunately for Wolves, due to the lack of a precise camera angle to determine whether Nunes was in an offside position when receiving the ball from the clearance, VAR could not overturn the decision made by the on-field referee who had raised the flag. This left many spectators frustrated and questioning the effectiveness of VAR. The incident highlighted the limitations of VAR when crucial camera angles are unavailable, leading to frustration and dissatisfaction among fans, and rightly so.

Liverpool's fortunate escape in the match against Wolves left some fans with mixed emotions. While the controversial decision saved them from defeat, the prospect of a replay was more disheartening, especially considering the disappointing performance and the thought of witnessing it again.

Brighton 3 - 0 Liverpool

Premier League
Saturday, 14th January 2023
Amex Stadium

You know the drill by now. This season was becoming even more of a write-off. Credit should be given to Brighton for their impressive performance. They displayed great organisation, skill, and cohesion on the field, showcasing the effective coaching of Roberto De Zerbi. Brighton thoroughly deserved their victory and showed the ability that exists within their team.

Brighton's midfield five, consisting of Kaoru Mitoma, Solly March, Alexis Mac Allister, Adam Lallana, and Moisés Caicedo, were outstanding in their performance against Liverpool. They demonstrated great control, passing accuracy, and understanding of each other's movements, reminiscent of the tiki-taka midfield trio of Xavi, Iniesta, and Busquets from Barcelona's golden era. Mitoma's presence on the left wing caused significant problems for Liverpool's defence, putting pressure on Trent Alexander-Arnold and Joël Matip throughout the game.

With his exceptional ball control, Adam Lallana showed his ability to retain possession in tight areas and make intelligent passes, as he did during his time at Liverpool. Solly March's brace was well-deserved, highlighting his effectiveness in scoring *and* creating goal-scoring opportunities. Alexis Mac Allister and Moisés Caicedo provided solidity and control in midfield, taking advantage of the vulnerabilities in Liverpool's midfield unit. All five of them were brilliant.

Looking at the attacking momentum graph, you will be able to see how dominant Brighton was throughout the match. The statistics further highlight Brighton's dominance and Liverpool's struggles. With only 38% possession compared to Brighton's 62%, Liverpool found themselves chasing the game and unable to establish control. The fact that Liverpool managed just two shots on target throughout the match, both of which came in the second half, indicated their lack of attacking threat and difficulties in creating scoring opportunities.

Liverpool was facing an uphill battle to recover from this dismal state. The team grappled with numerous issues, making a quick turnaround seem unlikely. The January transfer window had closed without significant reinforcements, much to the disappointment of supporters who had hoped for some much-needed additions. Injuries had dealt a heavy blow to Liverpool's squad, further complicating their season. The absence of key players like Diogo Jota, Luis Díaz, Roberto Firmino, and Darwin Núñez left a void in the team's attacking lineup. The strain of constant matches and the relentless schedule would test the team's depth and resilience even more. It felt like it couldn't possibly get any worse.

The match turned in Brighton's favour early in the second half when Liverpool's defensive lapse resulted in a costly goal. Joël Matip's misplaced pass in a dangerous area allowed Brighton to counterattack and exploit the space quickly. Solly March capitalised on the chance, finding himself in the correct position at the back post to tap the ball into the net.

Liverpool's woes continued as Brighton extended their lead in the fifty-third minute, with Solly March *again* finding the back of the net. The defensive organisation between Joël Matip and Ibrahima Konaté seemed disjointed, allowing Evan Ferguson to exploit the gap between them and play a well-timed through ball to March. The Brighton winger showed composure and skill to finish the chance, leaving Liverpool with a daunting two-goal deficit.

It was a frustrating moment for Liverpool, who found it challenging to make an impact on the match and struggled to break down Brighton's defence. The closest Liverpool came to scoring was when Trent Alexander-Arnold played a ball into the box, which Cody Gakpo couldn't make clean contact with.

I felt sorry for Gakpo. He must have wondered what he had come into with the team being so poor. With Darwin Núñez out with a hamstring issue, Gakpo became the central player in Liverpool's front three. He received no service throughout the whole match, Trent's pass aside. The expectation to perform was already too large for a new player, who should be doing something other than shouldering the responsibility this early in his Liverpool career.

Brighton's third goal added insult to injury for Liverpool, leaving the fans feeling even more disheartened. The Brighton supporters had been taunting Liverpool with chants of 'Ole' for every successful pass, and the situation turned even more embarrassing when Danny Welbeck added the cherry on top. It all started from a Brighton throw-in, with Solly March cleverly flicking the ball into the box for Welbeck to pounce on. In a swift display of skill, Welbeck expertly lifted the ball over the advancing Joe Gomez with his first touch before calmly slotting it past Alisson at the near post with his second touch. The goal was the final blow, completing the humiliation for Liverpool and compounding their frustration and disappointment.

While Jürgen Klopp has often taken responsibility for the team's poor performances in the past, he addressed the players' responsibility in his post-match press conference, which felt significant. While Klopp deserves some criticism for the team's form, holding the players accountable for their repeated underwhelming performances was crucial. The approach of diverting attention away from the players needed reconsidering, as it wasn't yielding the desired results. It was time for the players to step up, take ownership of their performances, and strive to improve the team's form. The following was taken from Klopp's post-match interview.

I'm not sure if it's because the game was only a few minutes ago, but I can't remember a worse game. Honestly, I can't, and I mean all, not only Liverpool. I can't remember. And that's my responsibility. That makes it a real low point for the moment. The problems are the same as last week, like we spoke about, we don't win the key battles on the pitch, the key challenges, and we give the ball away too easily.

That makes it difficult to organise protection for losing balls you should not lose. It's not easy, but it's fully my responsibility because I had an idea with a different formation, and that didn't work out. Sorry.

During the post-match press conference, James Pearce from The Athletic asked Klopp about the players' openness to the manager's advice, considering the recurring performance issues. Klopp responded by expressing his uncertainty about whether the players actively chose not to listen to his instructions. Still, he mentioned that they clearly understood his message during the week leading up to the match. If we assume Klopp's assessment is accurate, it is disheartening to witness a lack of execution from the players, as it goes against the expected level of professionalism and commitment. The players' failure to meet expectations has frustrated Klopp and the supporters.

I have immense respect and loyalty towards Jürgen Klopp. I prioritise his influence at Liverpool Football Club over any individual player in the squad. Klopp's apology to the travelling fans at the end of the match, with his head down and hands raised in a prayer-like gesture, acknowledged his sorrow. It is clear that Klopp shared the fans' frustration and recognised the need for improved performances. Jürgen Klopp knows the fans deserved better. The truth is, Klopp deserved better too.

Wolves 0 - 1 Liverpool

FA Cup Third-Round Replay
Tuesday, 17th January 2023
Molineux Stadium

Despite the initial reluctance surrounding the match, it unexpectedly provided a much-needed boost for both the team and the fans. There were reservations about the game's significance, given Liverpool's recent struggles. However, it presented an opportunity for Jürgen Klopp to implement rotations and try a different approach, which proved beneficial in the grand scheme.

On paper, Liverpool opted for a reshuffled lineup in the FA Cup replay, fielding a weaker team compared to the previous encounter just ten days prior. However, these changes benefitted Liverpool, particularly in addressing the pressing need for fresh legs in the midfield. The inclusion of Stefan Bajčetić, Naby Keïta, and Thiago in the midfield injected a renewed sense of energy. Additionally, the dynamic duo of Harvey Elliott and Fábio Carvalho, operating as the wide attacking players flanking Cody Gakpo, brought youthful enthusiasm, contributing to an intensified pressing game and providing decent coverage in the midfield area.

Despite occasional misplaced passes, Stefan Bajčetić made a strong impression during the match. His energy and ability were a breath of fresh air in a midfield that had often lacked vitality. Bajčetić's performance left a positive impact on supporters. Bajčetić and Naby Keïta, shouldering much of the midfield workload, allowed Thiago to shine. We know Thiago's exceptional skills when playing in a cohesive Liverpool team, but he thrives even more when surrounded by energetic midfielders. Thiago's playmaking abilities rely on having space and runners in the midfield, which enables him to show his passing and creative talents, thereby making a meaningful contribution to the team.

Harvey Elliott delivered a player-of-the-match performance, displaying immense determination throughout the game. He played a pivotal role in leading Liverpool's high press, which proved successful. It was his exceptional goal that ultimately separated the two sides. As Elliott surged forward from a midfield position, the Wolves defenders continuously retreated, inadvertently creating more space for Elliott to run into and exploit. He recognised the opportunity and unleashed a magnificent left-footed strike from about thirty yards out. The shot caught Wolves goalkeeper José Sá off guard, resulting in a sublime goal that handed Liverpool the much-needed and deserved lead.

Although a narrow one-nil victory can be nerve-wracking, Liverpool did well to restrict Wolves' chances. The closest Wolves came to scoring were from a couple of direct Rúben Neves free-kicks. Defensively, Ibrahima Konaté and Joe Gomez performed admirably, showing their composure. Nat Phillips also made a notable contribution when he replaced James Milner. Speaking of Milner, he assumed the role of a vocal captain, displaying his leadership qualities and delivering a solid and professional performance, as we would expect from a seasoned and experienced player.

Another refreshing aspect of this match was Liverpool's ability to keep a clean sheet. Unlike previous games with significant gaps in the defence and midfield, which allowed the opposition to penetrate and exploit their lines easily, Liverpool appeared more organised and compact. Moving forward, Liverpool needed to maintain this standard throughout the season, making themselves solid and challenging to defeat.

Jürgen Klopp now faced a selection dilemma. Should he stick with the experienced but uninspiring midfield trio of

Fabinho, Jordan Henderson, and Thiago, or should he give opportunities to players like Stefan Bajčetić, Naby Keïta, or Harvey Elliott, who had shown energy and compatibility on the pitch? Interestingly, Liverpool's reward for their victory over Wolves and progression to the FA Cup fourth round was another trip to the Amex Stadium to face Brighton.

Liverpool 0 - 0 Chelsea

Premier League
Saturday, 21st January 2023
Anfield

Jürgen Klopp made the bold decision of fielding the midfield trio of Stefan Bajčetić, Naby Keïta, and Thiago once again, as they had impressed in the previous match against Wolves. This choice meant leaving more experienced players like Jordan Henderson and Fabinho on the bench. However, despite their strong showing earlier in the week, the selected midfield trio failed to make the desired impact in this game.

Liverpool's lacklustre performance was disappointing, especially considering the hope generated by their recent 1-0 victory against Wolves. The Wolves victory was anticipated to be a foundation for a more consistent winning streak and a turnaround in the season. However, it was evident that the team required more than just a few rotations to reverse their fortunes and regain their winning form.

One positive aspect of the match was Liverpool's ability to keep another clean sheet. However, there were moments when the clean sheet was under threat, such as Chelsea's disallowed goal by Kai Havertz in the third minute. VAR correctly ruled it out for offside, and this decision allowed Liverpool to maintain their defensive solidity and deny their opponents from finding the back of the net.

While there had been worse performances this season, the game against Chelsea was undoubtedly disappointing. The overall performance lacked energy and creativity, making it one of the more lacklustre displays. The defensive line, consisting of Joe Gomez and Ibrahima Konaté, performed well and showed solidity, but this defensive focus came at the expense of the attacking prowess. As a result, Liverpool struggled to find a balance that allowed them to be solid at the back and fluid in their attacking movements. There was a significant imbalance in this regard, and finding the correct ratio was crucial for the team going forward.

Following the match against Chelsea, an interesting aspect emerged regarding the toll last season took on the Liverpool squad. While Jürgen Klopp had previously highlighted concerns about physical fatigue due to the demanding schedule, Thiago shed light on the *mental* consequences experienced by the team. In a post-match interview, Thiago discussed how the intense campaign from the previous season had impacted the players mentally. This insight provided a deeper understanding of Liverpool's challenges and offered valuable context for their performances this season. Thiago said:

It's not just about physical stuff, it is something phycological because we were so close to winning everything, and we just touched it, but sadly it went away. In the bad moments, we have to be together as a team. Last season we had one of the greatest seasons I've ever had in my life. This season is not one of the best, but it doesn't matter. It is a challenge.

The players had been affected by the challenges and pressures of the previous season, and their mental struggles and exhaustion undoubtedly contributed to this season's shortcomings. In the past, Liverpool has sought external support, such as bringing in individuals like Sebastian Steudtner, a German surfer, to speak with the players and address mental pressures and anxiety within the squad and how to harness those feelings. Similar interventions could have been beneficial in helping the players overcome negative emotions and the lingering effects of past experiences, as Thiago referred to them, "scars." However, creating a safe and supportive environment for such explorations is crucial and ensuring no time constraints is vital. Implementing mental well-being strategies during the middle of a demanding season may present challenges, as the focus is primarily on performance and results. Finding the right timing to address possible mental anguish is crucial in helping the players regain their confidence and overcome any psychological barriers they may be feeling. I hope this is something Liverpool looks into during the summer break.

Considering the context, Klopp's description of the result as a 'little step' seemed appropriate. While it wasn't a result to celebrate, securing a draw rather than suffering a loss could be seen as a slight positive. Both Liverpool and Chelsea went through transitional phases this season, and the match reflected that. The lack of spark and intensity on the pitch was understandable, as both teams were in a position that did not reflect their usual standards. The match was a battle between two teams trying to find their form, ultimately ending in a draw.

Brighton 2 - 1 Liverpool

FA Cup Fourth Round
Sunday, 29th January 2023
Amex Stadium

Liverpool's elimination from the FA Cup added to the list of disappointments this season. The defeat against Brighton, sealed by Kaoru Mitoma's late winner, only added to the frustrations. Liverpool's early exits from the EFL Cup and now the FA Cup highlighted the team's challenges and almost certainly meant Liverpool would not be winning a trophy. Looking ahead, Liverpool had a tough Champions League tie against Real Madrid looming in the coming months, and the less said about that, the better.

There's no denying that Liverpool's defensive vulnerabilities had been a significant concern throughout the season. Jürgen Klopp and the coaching staff made tactical adjustments to address these issues, which impacted Liverpool's attacking threat, particularly from the full-back positions. In recent successful years, Liverpool had relied heavily on the attacking prowess of their full-backs, who have been instrumental in providing width, crossing, and creating scoring opportunities. However, the emphasis on defensive stability resulted in a more cautious approach from the full-backs, limiting their forward runs and reducing their impact in the attacking third. This trade-off between defensive solidity and attacking threat is a delicate balance that Klopp and the coaching staff must navigate. The aim was to find a tactical solution to maintaining defensive stability while reintegrating the full-backs' attacking ability.

Another noticeable aspect of the match was Liverpool's struggle to maintain possession in midfield. While the defenders and goalkeeper appeared comfortable on the ball, the moment it reached the midfield, Liverpool would lose the ball. The issue arose when the midfielders dropped deep to receive passes, often facing the defenders instead of positioning themselves to play forward. This repetitive issue was frustrating to watch, hindering the team's ability to launch attacks.

In fairness, there was some improvement in Liverpool's performance compared to their previous encounter with Brighton, despite the result remaining the same. Liverpool showed more competitiveness this time on the pitch, whereas the last game felt one-sided. Another notable positive from the match was the performance of Ibrahima Konaté, who displayed resilience and solidity in Liverpool's defence. He stood out as a reliable figure amidst the defensive challenges the team was facing. Additionally, Cody Gakpo seemed more settled in his role as he led Liverpool's front line, giving glimpses of his potential as the eventual replacement for Roberto Firmino.

Liverpool managed to break the deadlock and take a rare lead in the match when Harvey Elliott found the back of the net. Mohamed Salah assisted, setting up Elliott with a well-timed through ball. Despite the goalkeeper's attempt to save the shot, the ball hit the bottom corner, giving Liverpool a sense of relief and optimism. However, Brighton quickly responded and equalised, dampening Liverpool's lead.

Brighton's equalising goal had an element of fortune to it. After Trent Alexander-Arnold headed the ball out of the box from a corner, Tariq Lamptey seized the opportunity and unleashed a first-time shot from about twenty yards out. To Liverpool's misfortune, the shot deflected off Lewis Dunk, altering its direction and catching Alisson off guard. Despite his best efforts to react, Alisson could not readjust to prevent the ball from finding the back of the net. The deflection off Dunk added an element of luck to Brighton's goal, and it was a moment that left Liverpool feeling hard done by.

The match remained largely uneventful in the second half until the closing moments when Brighton capitalised on a free kick. The ball was delivered from a wide area and found its way to the back post where Pervis Estupiñán was positioned. Estupiñán then lofted the ball back into a dangerous area near the opposite post, where Kaoru Mitoma awaited. Mitoma showed excellent ball control, taking a deft touch to bring the ball under control and then cleverly flicking it up with his second touch, deceiving Joe Gomez. Mitoma then unleashed a powerful strike that sailed past Alisson into the net before the ball touched the ground.

Throughout the match, Mitoma proved to be a constant thorn in Liverpool's side, causing problems with his direct style of play, pace, and close control. His exceptional performance and injury-time goal made him a deserving match-winner. However, the late goal dealt a devastating blow to Liverpool, ending their hopes of retaining the trophy.

The substitutions by Liverpool in recent games, including this match against Brighton, had raised concerns as they appeared to harm the team's performance. Despite the introduction of experienced players like James Milner, Jordan Henderson, and Fabinho, the substitutions resulted in a regression rather than improvement. Several factors could have contributed to this issue, such as disrupted team unity, changes in tactics or simply individual players struggling to find their rhythm after entering the game. However, it was another issue to add to the list of things Liverpool needed to fix.

Fabinho's only contribution to the match was a reckless challenge on Brighton forward Evan Ferguson. Tackling from behind, Fabinho raked his studs down Ferguson's Achilles. He immediately realised the severity of the tackle, raising his hands in acknowledgement of its danger and anticipating a red-card dismissal. Surprisingly, the referee only brandished a yellow card, which undoubtedly warranted a red. Professional Game Match Officials Limited (PGMOL) later affirmed that Fabinho should have been punished for his appalling tackle. I don't believe it was intentional from Fabinho, but an example of how off the pace he was, which resulted in a dangerous late tackle.

February

2023

- Wolves (A) - 4th February - EPL - Page 236

- Everton (H) - 13th February - EPL - Page 242

- Newcastle (A) - 18th February - EPL - Page 248

- Real Madrid (H) - 21st February - UCL - Page 252

- Crystal Palace (A) - 25th February - EPL - Page 260

Wolves 3 - 0 Liverpool

Premier League
Saturday, 4th February 2023
Molineux Stadium

When you think things couldn't get any worse, Liverpool proves you wrong. This match was an absolute disaster. No individuals stood out, only abysmal displays from the entire Liverpool team. Wolves quickly secured a 2-0 lead within the opening twelve minutes, and once the second goal was conceded, the game seemed irreversible. Liverpool's tactical decisions were consistently flawed, and the squad's confidence was severely lacking. The team was trapped in a suffocating atmosphere, where every disappointing result and performance intensified the mounting pressure. The pressure was reaching a boiling point, and it seemed inevitable that an explosive outcome was on the horizon.

After this defeat, the season felt like it had reached a disappointing conclusion. In an ideal scenario, with supporters already looking at the summer transfer window for quality additions to the squad, it was hoped that Jürgen Klopp would be provided with substantial financial resources to start the much-needed rebuild. This would require a change in ownership for Liverpool, with new owners willing to invest generously in the squad and the club. FSG's current self-sufficient model may not align with the urgency of a rebuild, but I am happy to be proven wrong.

If Liverpool can acquire players without the constraints of the self-sufficient model, Jürgen Klopp needs to display ruthlessness. A thorough assessment of the squad is required, and any players deemed no longer capable of contributing to the Liverpool rebuild, regardless of their value or reputation, must be let go.

Additionally, those individuals who have disappointed Klopp, the club, and the fans throughout this season should be swiftly and decisively moved on from the team. There should be no hesitation in making these necessary changes for the good of the team's future. Either FSG needs to invest significant money, not from their pocket, from the riches the club earns for being one of the biggest clubs in the world, or they need to sell the club. It is as simple as that.

The release of the Deloitte Football Money League rankings highlighted Liverpool's impressive financial performance, placing them among the top-earning football clubs worldwide. With reported earnings of £594.3m from the

2021/22 season alone, Liverpool's revenue is undoubtedly substantial. However, it is perplexing that the club did not allocate any of these funds towards strengthening the midfield during the January transfer window. As per the rankings, the absence of reinforcements in an area of need was frustrating, especially considering the financial resources available. It felt neglectful to disregard improvements, given the club's circumstances.

Nevertheless, back to the defeat. Joël Matip's involvement in Wolves' first goal was a moment to forget for the Liverpool defender. As Hwang Hee-chan advanced towards a lofted-through ball, Matip's hesitancy allowed Hwang to gain an advantage in reaching the ball first. Whether it was an ill-timed attempt to play the offside trap or falling for a dummy, Matip's decision-making in that situation was questionable, leading to a breakdown in defensive cover. Following Hwang's attempt to cross the ball into the box, Matip's block inadvertently resulted in an unfortunate deflection that found its way into the bottom corner of the net. Despite the valiant efforts of Trent Alexander-Arnold and Alisson to clear the ball off the goal line, the goal was awarded to Wolves, putting them in the lead.

Seven minutes later, Liverpool's defensive woes continued as Joe Gomez made a costly mistake leading to another goal for Wolves. It started with a deep free-kick from Wolves, which Matheus Cunha managed to receive the ball and deliver a cross from the edge of the penalty area. Alisson came off his line to punch the ball away, but instead of clearing it, Joe Gomez headed the ball deeper into a dangerous area of the box. Alisson had likely called for the ball, but Gomez either didn't hear or ignored the goalkeeper's instructions.

The ball fell to Max Kilman, who was poised to score with a header. However, Cody Gakpo positioned himself well and made a crucial block, denying Kilman the opportunity. Unfortunately for Liverpool, the ball fell to Craig Dawson, making his debut, who unleashed a powerful shot that found the back of the net, extending Wolves' lead to two goals. These mistakes and lack of composure in crucial moments have been recurring issues throughout the season.

Despite a more promising start to the second half, Liverpool's efforts to get back into the game were met with frustration. The team displayed determination and controlled play, keeping Wolves in their half. However, despite their dominance, Liverpool couldn't convert their chances into goals. To add to their misery, Wolves capitalised on a counter-attack to extend their lead and make it three goals. This setback deflated Liverpool's hopes of mounting a comeback. It was a cruel turn of events considering their effort to regain control of the match.

Following a turnover in the midfield, João Moutinho dispossessed Stefan Bajčetić and quickly initiated a counter-attack by playing a through ball to Adama Traoré. Although the pass sent Traoré slightly wider than desired, he demonstrated composure by slowing down the play and waiting for his teammates to join the attack. Rúben Neves made a well-timed run towards the centre of the box, a threat that Thiago failed to recognise or react to. Traoré executed a simple side-foot pass to Neves, who had enough time and space to control the ball inside Liverpool's box before calmly slotting it into the bottom corner of the net. It was a culmination of defensive lapses that led to the third goal for Wolves. Raúl Jiménez had an opportunity to make it even worse for Liverpool, but his lobbed shot was misguided and comfortably collected by Alisson.

The hardest thing to take from this match was that the result didn't come as a surprise. Multiple fans predicted a tough time against Wolves, meaning they were no longer shocked when defeats like this occurred.

Liverpool 2 - 0 Everton

Premier League
Monday, 13th February 2023
Anfield

Jürgen Klopp gave the squad two days off following the disappointing loss to Wolves. Sometimes, after a tough defeat, it can be beneficial for players to take some time away from the training ground to regroup and refocus. The break can help them clear their minds and return with renewed energy and determination. However, the two-day break wasn't only to regain energy and motivation. Klopp said he didn't want to see the players' faces after the Wolves defeat, and I can completely empathise. I didn't want to see their faces either.

A whole week of training allowed Klopp and the coaching staff to address the issues that arose in the previous match and rectify them. This had a positive impact, as Liverpool showed signs of improvement. Training sessions allow the team to fine-tune their tactics and focus on improvement areas. Typically, when playing three matches a week, the focus is on recovery before playing the next match, limiting the chance to work on tactics during these busy periods.

It's often said that hope can be a double-edged sword, as it can lead to disappointment if expectations aren't met. Given the rollercoaster nature of the season, it was wise to approach each match cautiously, and the significance of this particular match cannot be understated. A loss could have created more pressure and negative attention, further dividing the fan base. Fortunately, Liverpool rose to the occasion, displaying confidence, rejuvenation, and determination, but mostly it provided a much-needed boost for everyone.

Much was said about the standout performance of Stefan Bajčetić in the match against Everton. Despite his young age, Bajčetić displayed composure and confidence while playing alongside experienced midfielders Jordan Henderson and Fabinho. With Fabinho returning to his defensive midfield role, Bajčetić was given a slightly more advanced position, allowing him to showcase his energy and contribute both in attack with his impressive passing and defence with crucial tackles.

Bajčetić's contribution to the team was remarkable, as evidenced by his exceptional work rate. Throughout the match, he covered a staggering distance of 11.14 kilometres, displaying his tireless effort and commitment. His ability to handle the pressure of such a significant occasion was equally impressive. Despite the weight of Liverpool's recent poor form and the high-stakes nature of the match against local rivals, Bajčetić remained composed and played a pivotal role in securing the victory. His outstanding performance did not go unnoticed by his teammates and the commentators. In Salah's post-match interview, he hailed Bajčetić as Liverpool's best player, recognising his impact on the game. Jamie Carragher, providing commentary for Sky Sports, awarded Bajčetić the player of the match, a well-deserved accolade for his performance.

Despite an early nervy moment from Joël Matip, Liverpool quickly found their rhythm and took control of the match. They dominated possession and dictated play in crucial areas of the pitch, showing a level of performance that had been missing in recent times. However, Everton managed to launch a rare attack and earned a corner. James Tarkowski rose highest from the resulting corner and directed a header towards the goal, only to see it strike the post. Liverpool reacted quickly to clear the rebound and swiftly initiated a counter-attack.

It was Darwin Núñez who played a clever one-two exchange with Mohamed Salah on the edge of Liverpool's box, creating space for Núñez to carry the ball up the left flank. With Salah and Cody Gakpo making central runs, Núñez spotted their movement and delivered a pass into the centre. Unexpectedly, Jordan Pickford, Everton's goalkeeper, anticipated the pass going to Gakpo and adjusted his position accordingly to save a potential Gakpo shot. However, Salah reached the ball and, with a stretched leg, guided it into the empty net, giving Liverpool the lead. It was a crucial moment that rewarded Liverpool's dominance and gave them an advantage in the match.

Liverpool's second goal showed us their trademark attacking style, with the fullbacks playing a crucial role in the build-up. As Salah made a penetrating run down the right flank, Trent Alexander-Arnold executed an overlapping run, providing an option for Salah's pass. Trent received the ball and delivered a low cross to the back post, where Gakpo was positioned to tap it into the net.

Not anticipating a Liverpool player behind him, Conor Coady failed to clear the ball, assuming it would either be gathered by Pickford or roll out for a goal kick. This allowed Gakpo to pounce on the loose ball and score. The goal bolstered Gakpo's confidence, and he continued to show his skills by dribbling past opponents and driving Liverpool's attack forward. The involvement of Trent Alexander-Arnold and Andrew Robertson in the build-up highlighted the importance of Liverpool's fullbacks in the attack. Liverpool becomes more dangerous when the fullbacks venture forward and contribute to the team's offensive moves.

A memorable incident involving Andrew Robertson and Jordan Pickford occurred during the match. As Robertson was advancing with the ball, he was flagged offside by the assistant referee, and upon hearing the whistle, he playfully kicked the ball away from Pickford, who had come out to collect it and restart the game. In response, Pickford bumped into Robertson with his chest, creating a laughable moment on the pitch. Robertson couldn't help but laugh in Pickford's face at his attempt to be aggressive, and even Pickford saw the funny side and smiled.

While it was necessary to remain cautious and not get carried away with this victory, appreciating and savouring the positive aspects was also required. This campaign has taught us not to take wins for granted, as they have been hard to come by. Despite the challenges, there were small reasons for optimism, such as the improved performance and the return of key players like Diogo Jota and Roberto Firmino. Additionally, having Virgil van Dijk back on the bench signified progress in terms of squad fitness. When everything clicked, there was a small glimpse of what Liverpool could do. We just needed it to click more often.

A few hours before the match, the leaked Independent Review Panel report shed light on the events surrounding the UEFA Champions League final held in Paris last season. The report confirmed what we already knew - that Liverpool fans were *not* responsible for the incidents. Instead, the report placed the blame on UEFA and the French authorities. The report *commended* Liverpool fans for their composed response, preventing a potential disaster despite the mistreatment they endured. Their collective calmness and resilience, influenced by past tragedies, played a crucial role in ensuring all safety and, importantly, avoiding fatalities.

Newcastle Utd. 0 - 2 Liverpool

Premier League
Saturday, 18th February 2023
St. James' Park

Liverpool's back-to-back victories were a breath of fresh air. Although the match at St. James' Park wasn't as aesthetically pleasing as the previous game against Everton, the result is what truly mattered. Facing a challenging early evening kick-off in Newcastle with passionate home fans, Liverpool rose to the occasion. They silenced the crowd, maintained composure, and completed their objective of winning three points.

Trent Alexander-Arnold's return to form as an assist provider was a welcome sight. Just as he did against Everton, he delivered a perfectly floated ball, this time to Darwin Núñez, who made no mistake finding the back of the net. Núñez's goal showed his characteristic style of powerful strikes rather than finesse finishes, as noted by Jamie Carragher during his commentary. While Carragher's comments may have sounded critical, the important thing is that Núñez keeps scoring, which we will all be pleased about.

Shortly after, Liverpool extended their lead as Cody Gakpo found the back of the net with a clinical finish. Mohamed Salah provided the assist with a delightful lofted through ball, perfectly timed for Gakpo's run. Gakpo showed great composure, taking a touch inside the box before calmly placing the ball past the onrushing Nick Pope.

Liverpool found themselves in an even more advantageous position when Newcastle's goalkeeper, Pope, was shown a red card for a moment of madness. It occurred after Alisson collected a Newcastle free-kick and swiftly launched a long pass to release Salah on a potential goal-scoring opportunity. Pope, sensing the danger, rushed out of his box to clear the ball, but his clearance went awry, and he intentionally handled the ball well outside his penalty area. The referee had no option but to give a red card, leaving Pope to rue his actions and miss out on the upcoming Carabao Cup Final between Newcastle and Manchester United. This situation led to Loris Karius starting the final for Newcastle, a final in which they lost.

The first twenty-two minutes of the match were eventful, with Liverpool scoring two goals and Newcastle being reduced to ten men. It was essential for Liverpool not to blow their advantage, as a loss from this position would have been disastrous. However, despite Newcastle's efforts to claw their way back into the game, Liverpool emerged as the victors. Credit must be given to Allan Saint-Maximin, who posed a constant threat with his skill and direct approach. Despite being on the losing side, he was recognised as the player of the match, highlighting his excellent performance.

In some aspects, the red card for Pope had a detrimental impact on the match. It disrupted the flow and forced Liverpool to adopt a more cautious approach, focusing on ball possession to control the game. While the early goals allowed Liverpool to establish control, Newcastle still created opportunities, requiring Alisson to make crucial saves to maintain a clean sheet.

Once again, Alisson showcased his world-class abilities and proved to be Liverpool's standout player. His exceptional goalkeeping skills and quick reactions prevented several potential goals for the opposition. It is essential to appreciate Alisson's immense value to the team, as Liverpool would be significantly worse without him between the posts.

Overall, the Reds' performance wasn't flawless, and some areas still needed improvement. However, the ability to adapt while securing a victory was a significant step forward for Liverpool, considering their recent struggles. Learning from each match and progressing along the way was essential. The change to Newcastle's game plan due to the red card certainly impacted Liverpool's performance, and it is vital to consider that. Ultimately, as long as Liverpool kept winning games, there was room for optimism. However, Real Madrid was the next opponent, and they would prove to be a much tougher test.

Liverpool 2 - 5 Real Madrid

UEFA Champions League R-16, First Leg
Tuesday, 21st February 2023
Anfield

While it's true that Real Madrid is widely regarded as one of the top clubs in European football, with a rich history and a tradition of success, it didn't make this defeat feel any better. Despite any changes to their squad, with transfers both in and out of the club, Real Madrid consistently remains a solid and well-organised team, showing their elite stature. However, acknowledging Real Madrid's impressive ability to stay at the top doesn't lessen the disappointment of the defeat.

Recent results, including the victories against Everton and Newcastle, may have led us to believe we could challenge and compete against top teams like Real Madrid. The excitement and momentum from those wins closed our eyes to the difficulties we would face against such an established opponent. While Liverpool scored twice in the match, it became clear that the task was more challenging than we realised. The reality of the result showed the gap that still existed between us and the very best in European football, primarily due to how far we had fallen.

Darwin Núñez opened the scoring with a brash back-heel finish to open the scoring. While I sometimes hope for a more straightforward finish, it's hard to argue with the effectiveness of Núñez's confident move. Núñez showed determination by running past Madrid's defender Éder Militão and getting in front of him to connect with the cross. It was brave to opt for flair and execute the back-heel finish instead of a more straightforward side-footed shot. Regardless, Núñez's goal demonstrated his striker's instinct and willingness to take risks to find the back of the net. Mohamed Salah also deserves credit for his contribution to this opening goal, as he provided a well-timed pass to find Núñez in the box.

Liverpool must have felt incredibly fortunate when Thibaut Courtois made a rare mistake that led to their second goal. Courtois had performed remarkably against Liverpool in the previous season's UEFA Champions League Final, earning the Player of the Match award and helping his team win the trophy. However, in this match, Courtois made a rare mistake. In the fourteenth minute, a high back-pass from Dani Carvajal found its way to Courtois. The goalkeeper initially controlled the ball with his chest, but as he tried to bring it under control with his feet, the ball inadvertently struck his knee, causing it to rebound into the path of Salah. Capitalising on the goalkeeper's error, Salah swiftly pressed Courtois and hit the loose ball into the net, extending Liverpool's lead to two goals early in the game.

Real Madrid displayed remarkable composure despite being two goals down. Unlike Liverpool, who might have crumbled under similar circumstances, Madrid remained composed and calm. Their experience and previous successes in high-pressure situations allowed them to stay focused and determined.

Vinícius Júnior's goal was a standout moment in the match and widely regarded as the game's best goal. Considering the seven-goal spectacle, this speaks volumes about the quality of Vinícius' strike. It was a goal that seemed almost impossible to score. Surrounded by Liverpool defenders, including Joe Gomez, Fabinho, Trent Alexander-Arnold, and Jordan Henderson, Vinícius unleashed a powerful shot that found the bottom corner of the net, leaving Alisson with little chance of saving it.

Steve McManaman, providing co-commentary for BT Sport, mentioned the need to close down Vinícius quicker. However, the truth was that Vinícius demonstrated exceptional skill and composure in a small pocket of space and scored a brilliant goal despite the multiple Liverpool players around him. Closing him down quicker didn't look like it would have made much of a difference.

Real Madrid's equalising goal resulted from an unfortunate mistake by Alisson. The sequence began with Stefan Bajčetić losing possession in midfield while attempting to dribble past Karim Benzema and Federico Valverde instead of opting for a safer backpass to Virgil van Dijk. Valverde then played a well-executed through ball to Vinícius, but Joe Gomez provided defensive cover and played a back-pass to Alisson to halt the Real Madrid attack.

There were some criticisms of Gomez's back-pass, which were unjustified. Although Gomez had a less-than-stellar game overall, his back-pass to Alisson was fine. The ball rolled towards Alisson's favoured right foot, and he attempted to return the pass to Gomez. Unfortunately, his return pass struck Vinícius and ended up floating into the net, resulting in an unfortunate mistake. It was tough to see Liverpool concede in this manner, as it was a significant mistake on Alisson's part, levelling the game at 2-2.

At this stage of the match, both goalkeepers had made costly mistakes that led to goals. Despite Liverpool's early two-goal lead, the game was now level. While Liverpool could have bemoaned their lost advantage, they were still in the match and had an opportunity to regroup and reassess their approach. With better in-game management, they could have potentially settled for a draw and aimed to perform better in the return leg at the Bernabéu in a few weeks. However, the second-half performance by Liverpool was a significant collapse, severely diminishing their chances of progressing in the competition. The outcome of the first leg pointed towards Liverpool's exit from the tournament.

Real Madrid wasted no time taking the lead with their third goal of the night. Early in the second half, Joe Gomez committed a foul near the edge of Liverpool's penalty area. Luka Modrić stepped up to take the resulting free-kick and delivered a well-placed ball into the box at chest height. Éder Militão was left unmarked as he calmly headed the ball into the net. Liverpool's zonal marking system proved ineffective, as no defenders reacted or tried to challenge Militão. It was poor defending and stood out as one of the worst goals conceded by Liverpool in the match. The Militão goal highlighted Liverpool players' lack of movement and organisation. It was a truly disappointing and shambolic defensive lapse. No Liverpool player moved, making it much easier for Militão to score.

Rafael Benítez provided punditry for Sky Sports a few days before this match against Real Madrid, and Benítez expressed his concerns about Liverpool's defensive problems. He highlighted that if Liverpool defended poorly against Real Madrid, Vinícius and Benzema would likely find the back of the net. Unfortunately for Liverpool, Benítez's prediction was about to come true, with Benzema adding to the damage.

Following a neat exchange with Vinícius at the edge of Liverpool's box, Karim Benzema unleashed a relatively tame shot towards the goal. However, the shot took a fortunate deflection off Gomez, leaving Alisson caught off guard as he had already anticipated the original direction of the ball. It was undeniably a lucky goal, but for Benzema, the manner of the goal didn't matter as it extended Real Madrid's lead to 4-2 at Anfield. But Benzema wasn't satisfied with just one goal. He went on to score another, thanks to an impressive display of playmaking by Modrić.

The 37-year-old Ballon d'Or winner intercepted a pass from Fabinho following a poor touch and swiftly advanced towards an exposed Liverpool backline. With only Virgil van Dijk as the lone defender, Modrić had Vinícius on his left and

Benzema on his right, charging alongside him. Modrić played the ball to Vinícius, who then passed it to Benzema. With a clever dummy shot that deceived Alisson and caused him to commit, Benzema smoothly manoeuvred around the goalkeeper, placing the ball calmly into the empty net. Though Virgil was on the line, there was no stopping Benzema's composed finish. The humiliation for Liverpool was now complete.

A second leg remained to be played at the Bernabéu on March 15, but given the significant scoreline in the first leg, Liverpool's chances of overturning the defeat seemed slim. The performances throughout the season hadn't given me any optimism regarding Liverpool's ability to stage a comeback. Truthfully, the supporters knew Liverpool was out of the Champions League after the first-leg result.

Toward the end of the match, memories of Liverpool's loss to Barcelona at Camp Nou in 2019 resurfaced in my mind. However, it wasn't because I believed Liverpool could replicate that incredible feat and overturn a 3-0 deficit in the second leg. Instead, it reminded me of Jurgen Klopp's inspiring words to his team after that challenging defeat: 'If anyone can overturn this, it's you guys.' Unfortunately, *this* Liverpool team lacked the resilience and ability to produce a comeback. It was disheartening to see the contrast between the squad that achieved that memorable triumph, and the team that lost 5-2 at home against Real Madrid, despite consisting of several of the same players.

Crystal Palace 0 - 0 Liverpool

Premier League
Saturday, 25th February 2023
Selhurst Park

This match faded quickly from memory, leaving us disappointed and with a wasted Saturday night. The clash between Liverpool and Crystal Palace proved to be one of the most forgettable encounters of the season. It lacked any spark or excitement, offering ninety minutes of sheer boredom and frustration. My heart goes to the dedicated fans who go to great lengths, waking up at ridiculous hours due to time differences and kick-off times, only to witness such a lacklustre display. Their commitment deserves better, and I sympathise with those who had to rise in the middle of the night to endure this disappointing match.

Jürgen Klopp opted for several changes in the starting lineup to maintain freshness within the team. Diogo Jota, returning after a lengthy absence, featured in the starting eleven. Naby Keïta also returned to the team, while Joël Matip partnered Virgil Van Dijk at centre-back in place of the injured and struggling Joe Gomez. James Milner was handed a starting role as well. Despite these alterations, the rotations failed to bring about any significant impact. In the final third, Liverpool's performance lacked creativity and a clinical touch, resulting in a lacklustre and uneventful game.

Despite having Fabinho and Stefan Bajčetić available as options on the bench, Jordan Henderson was deployed in the defensive midfield position for this match. This has been seen before, and it has often proven to be ineffective. Henderson's role in the defensive midfield can be dull to watch. He prioritises safety, opting for simple sideways passes and rarely taking risks or attempting defence-splitting passes.

Unfortunately, as of late, Henderson also lacks the necessary mobility, creativity, and stamina for this deeper midfield role, which has affected his recent performances. While his style may be acceptable when Liverpool is winning and looking to preserve the lead, seeing Henderson in the defensive midfield position during a drawn game can be frustrating. His most notable involvement in the match was unintentionally blocking Trent Alexander-Arnold's promising free-kick attempt near the edge of the box that looked certain to hit the back of the net.

Naby Keïta had a particularly disappointing first half of the match, struggling to make a positive impact. He received a yellow card and continuously committed fouls, pushing the boundaries of the referee's patience. His passing was inaccurate, and he failed to contribute significantly to the team. Keïta's statistics, such as winning only two out of ten ground duels and giving away possession seven times, further proved his poor performance. It was unsurprising when Klopp decided to substitute him at half-time, bringing on Harvey Elliott in his place.

It was becoming increasingly apparent that Keïta's time at Liverpool was ending. His tenure with the club has been marred by frequent injuries, which have limited his availability and added to the frustrations surrounding his performances. Based on his display against Palace, Keïta's commitment and focus appeared elsewhere, likely contemplating his next move in the summer transfer window when he leaves Liverpool for free.

Many argue that it was best for both parties to part ways. Liverpool needs players fully invested in the team's success, and Keïta's inconsistent performances and availability issues suggested his time at Liverpool was close to ending. In June 2022, it was confirmed that Keïta had joined the German side Werder Bremen, taking a significant pay cut to join. The Bremen medical staff were sceptical about his ability to pass the medical tests, but he passed easily. The scepticism they had, however, said it all.

Crystal Palace had a golden opportunity to score when Liverpool made a costly mistake. It was a frustratingly familiar scenario, as Liverpool's players seemed uneasy and made errors in possession. In particular, Trent Alexander-Arnold and Joël Matip appeared nervous, and Trent inadvertently gifted the ball to Palace striker Jean-Philippe Mateta. Mateta's resulting shot, however, lacked power and failed to trouble Alisson significantly. Later, Mateta had another chance when Jeffrey Schlupp dispossessed Trent and passed the ball to the French striker. Mateta's effort struck the crossbar, marking Palace's most promising goal-scoring opportunity. A more clinical striker would have punished Liverpool twice, but fortunately for the Reds, Mateta couldn't capitalise on these chances.

Liverpool had a few notable chances to score, but they could not find the back of the net. Diogo Jota came closest when he attempted a shot from a tight angle at the back post, only to see his header hit the outside of the post. Mohamed Salah also had a decent opportunity when he curled a left-footed shot that struck the crossbar. These moments provided glimpses of Liverpool's attacking threat, but ultimately, they couldn't convert their chances into goals.

One positive takeaway from the match was that Liverpool avoided a defeat and kept a clean sheet. While Crystal Palace's lack of attacking prowess may lessen the significance of the clean sheet, it was still an accomplishment to prevent any goals from being conceded. In a season where Liverpool had faced defensive challenges, not conceding a goal could be seen as a step in the right direction.

This performance further emphasised the understanding that Liverpool required a significant overhaul during the upcoming summer transfer window. To facilitate this, the club would benefit from a financial boost provided by the owners. However, in a recent interview with the Boston Sports Journal, John W. Henry clarified that Liverpool Football Club was *not* for sale, though the search for potential investors continued.

If the desired investment is not secured, there may be doubts regarding the current owners' commitment to providing the funds required for rebuilding. The fanbase will express their discontent and frustration if Liverpool fails to make substantial financial investments and undertake a squad rebuild. There is no more room for complacency.

Liverpool needs signings, and anything but that is unforgivable.

March
2023

- Wolves (H) - 1st March - EPL - Page 268

- Man. United (H) - 5th March - EPL - Page 273

- Bournemouth (A) - 11th March - EPL - Page 280

- Real Madrid (A) - 15th March - UCL - Page 284

Liverpool 2 - 0 Wolves

Premier League
Wednesday, 1st March 2023
Anfield

Liverpool's victory against Wolves may not have been the most aesthetically pleasing, but the most important aspect was getting the job done and earning the crucial three points. The football adage that winning becomes a habit is often repeated for a reason, highlighting the importance of maintaining positive momentum. At this stage of the season, the focus was primarily on accumulating three points regularly, even if it meant grinding out results. So, accepting and embracing such gritty victories became essential.

Liverpool's run of ten points from their last four Premier League matches was a positive sign, especially considering the clean sheets they had kept during this period. While the draw against Crystal Palace was disappointing, viewing it in the context of progress was essential. The team's undefeated streak remained intact, which was more critical than a defeat.

It's also worth mentioning that the season presented a different challenge for Liverpool, as they are not competing at the top of the table against a financially doped juggernaut (allegedly). The level of form required to compete at that elite level is undeniably demanding. However, in the race for a top-four finish, Liverpool didn't necessarily need to be flawless, as other teams vying for the same positions would inevitably drop points. Adjusting to this mindset was challenging, especially for a club used to competing at the top of the league for a considerable period.

Darwin Núñez returned to the starting lineup after recovering from a shoulder injury that had sidelined him for the previous match against Crystal Palace. Diogo Jota took up the central role in the front three, allowing Cody Gakpo to have a well-deserved rest. Kostas Tsimikas, Harvey Elliott, and Stefan Bajčetić also returned to the first team, along with Ibrahima Konaté.

As mentioned, the performance left room for improvement, particularly in the first half, which was somewhat lacklustre and uneventful. Liverpool's most promising opportunities came through Harvey Elliott, who had two notable chances. The first was a headed shot that he directed wide, which he should have done better with. The second chance was an on-target shot that forced Wolves' goalkeeper José Sá to make a good save. While there were occasional instances of indecisiveness at the back from Liverpool, thankfully, it did not result in conceding a goal.

In the second half, Liverpool intensified their efforts to find a goal. Darwin Núñez appeared to have scored, but the goal was disallowed after a VAR review. Diogo Jota showed incredible dribbling skills as he weaved through the Wolverhampton defence, creating chaos in the box. Nélson Semedo resorted to pushing Jota to halt his progress, leading to a loose ball. Darwin Núñez seized the opportunity and skillfully placed the ball into the far bottom corner of the net. However, VAR intervened, prompting referee Paul Tierney to review the incident on the pitch-side screen. Upon review, Tierney determined that Jota's stumble, as a result of Semedo's challenge, resulted in Wolves' defender Max Kilman slipping and impeding his ability to challenge Núñez for the ball. Despite the contention that Semedo caused Jota's stumble, the referee remained unsympathetic and disallowed the goal.

The controversial decision served as a spark, fueling Liverpool's determination to salvage a positive outcome from the match. Inside Anfield, the noise levels rose as the crowd rallied in defiance, refusing to let the disallowed goal dampen their spirits. The players responded with resilience, unwilling to let the ruling cost them a victory. Virgil Van Dijk ultimately broke the deadlock, capitalising from a Liverpool free-kick. Trent Alexander-Arnold delivered a lofted ball into the box, which Virgil met with a powerful header, forcing José Sá into making a save. The Portuguese goalkeeper could only parry the ball weakly, allowing Diogo Jota to swiftly strike it back across the six-yard box for Virgil to head home into the relatively unguarded net. It was a goal that Virgil couldn't miss, and the relief in his celebration spoke volumes after the earlier denied goal.

Four minutes later, Mohamed Salah extended the lead. After being substituted onto the field, Cody Gakpo executed a quick one-two pass with Kostas Tsimikas, who had plenty of room on the left flank to surge forward. Tsimikas advanced towards the goal line and delivered a cross into the box. Salah, displaying great agility and quick thinking, directed the ball with his thigh to find the back of the net. The second goal provided Liverpool with a safety net and maintained their advantage for the remainder of the match.

Things were heading in the right direction, but some areas still required refinement. Maintaining clean sheets effectively avoids defeat, so it was essential to continue that trend. The upcoming match against Manchester United at Anfield on

Sunday, March 5, presented a more significant challenge. United arrived at Anfield full of confidence, having clinched the Carabao Cup, triumphed over Barcelona in the Europa League, and secured a spot in the FA Cup quarter-finals. Ex-United players turned pundits were left red-faced with their pre-match predictions, providing a delightful spectacle for football fans. However, the match's outcome surpassed all expectations and will be remembered as the standout result of the season, etching its place in the history books forever.

"I do feel this is a Liverpool [team] that this Manchester United team could damage." - **Gary Neville**

"Nervous? This is the most confident I've been going into a Liverpool game for probably the last six or seven years." - **Rio Ferdinand**

Liverpool 7 - 0 Manchester Utd.

Premier League
Sunday, 5th March 2023
Anfield

Let's set the record straight. This was an unprecedented and unimaginable outcome. Scorelines of this magnitude against intense rivals are a rarity and something that may not be witnessed again in our lifetimes. It was a moment to savour, to fully immerse ourselves in, and to etch into our memories: a resounding victory over our long-standing rivals. For those of us who grew up in the shadow of Manchester United's continuous triumphs, which seemed to overshadow our hopes and dreams, this result holds a special significance. It served as a balm, a soothing remedy for our years of disappointment and heartache, watching them win everything repeatedly. So we needed to bask in the glory of this achievement, relish every aspect of it, and forever cherish this monumental scoreline against our old enemies.

Pundits and fans associated with Manchester United started believing their hype. After winning the Carabao Cup the weekend before this match, Manchester United was riding high, which made it even sweeter to witness Liverpool scoring seven past this United team and bringing them back down to earth with an almighty crash. Liverpool humiliated Manchester United, delivering a much-needed reality check and showcasing that Liverpool Football Club can still create unforgettable moments.

The contention in the build-up to this match was the inclusion of Harvey Elliott ahead of Stefan Bajčetić. Bajčetić was the in-form player, but doubts were quickly put to rest. Every player on the pitch, including Elliott, displayed superb professionalism and proved that Liverpool was superior. The match started with great intensity from Liverpool, although they couldn't convert their early dominance into goals. Manchester United gradually grew into the game, and it seemed like the first half would end with a level scoreline. However, Andy Robertson and Cody Gakpo had other ideas and turned the game in Liverpool's favour before the halftime whistle.

Darwin Núñez struggled during the first forty-five minutes as the left winger. However, a tactical change late in the first half saw Núñez and Cody Gakpo swapping positions. With Gakpo now on the left wing, Robertson dribbled towards the centre of the pitch, creating space. Spotting the opportunity, Robertson stopped the ball and signalled for Gakpo to run behind Fred, who had dropped back to cover the right-back position. Robertson's pass was executed perfectly, allowing Gakpo to take a touch past Raphaël Varane, who was closing him down. With his second touch, he expertly curled a low and powerful shot beyond David De Gea's reach. It was a great goal from Gakpo, giving Liverpool a well-deserved lead just before halftime and providing them with a crucial advantage going into the break.

The second half began, and Liverpool immediately stepped up their performance. A pivotal moment came when Fabinho won a contested ball against Casemiro near the edge of the Manchester United box. Fabinho skillfully flicked a through ball to Mohamed Salah, who attempted to deliver a cross into the box. However, the ball deflected off Luke Shaw and fell favourably for Harvey Elliott. Without hesitation, Elliott struck the ball first-time into the air, directing it perfectly onto the head of Darwin Núñez, who had an easy task of heading it into the net. Núñez's instinctual finish extended Liverpool's lead to two goals.

Moments later, it was Gakpo's time to shine once again. Salah displayed incredible skill and agility, completely outwitting Lisandro Martínez and confusing the United defender. Martínez slipped as he attempted to anticipate Salah's movements as the Egyptian effortlessly evaded him. Salah then played a simple yet perfectly timed pass to release Gakpo, who found himself one-on-one with De Gea. With composure and finesse, Gakpo delicately chipped the ball over De Gea from a tight angle, adding a third goal to Liverpool's tally. It was a sublime display of teamwork combined with individual brilliance, making the goal look effortless for Salah and Gakpo.

Despite already leading 3-0 against a fierce rival early in the second half, Liverpool showed no signs of slowing down. They were determined to make a resounding statement, leaving no doubts about their superiority over Manchester United. It was a display of ruthlessness and a desire to humiliate their opposition, proving to everyone who thought that this United team had surpassed Liverpool that they were mistaken. The Reds continued their relentless assault, showcasing their dominance and leaving no room for doubt or mercy.

Liverpool's fourth goal was a result of a swift counter-attack. Darwin Núñez initiated the move, dribbling down the left wing with Gakpo, Salah, and Elliott positioned ahead of him. As Núñez attempted to pass the ball to Elliott, Scott McTominay intervened, intercepting the pass. Fortunately for Liverpool, the ball fell back to Núñez, who made another attempt to play a pass. McTominay's interception was not as lucky this time, deflecting the ball perfectly into Salah's path. With ample space in the centre of the box, Salah swiftly turned and unleashed a ferocious half-volley that struck the underside of the crossbar, leaving David De Gea helpless. It was an unstoppable and thunderous strike from Salah, matching Robbie Fowler's record for the most goals scored by a Liverpool player in the Premier League.

Liverpool extended their lead to five goals with yet another header from Darwin Núñez. Following a corner kick, Jordan Henderson ventured out wide to retrieve the ball after Manchester United had initially cleared the danger. With composure, Henderson delivered a beautifully curled cross into the box. Núñez timed his jump perfectly and directed the ball into the net with the side of his head, showcasing his aerial ability for the second time in the match. It was a well-executed goal, adding to Liverpool's commanding lead.

Salah continued his remarkable performance by scoring Liverpool's sixth goal and surpassing Robbie Fowler as the club's all-time leading scorer in the Premier League. The opportunity arose from a deflected clearance attempt by Luke Shaw, which fell kindly for Salah in a central position. With his trademark poise and precision, Salah unleashed a sweeping right-footed strike that found the back of the net. It was a significant milestone for Salah, who achieved this feat in just six seasons with the club. His impact and the records he has broken during his tenure at Liverpool have been extraordinary. Salah's contributions have firmly established him as a Liverpool legend.

In a poignant moment, Roberto Firmino capped off the scoring with Liverpool's seventh goal. Earlier in the week, Firmino had announced his summer departure from Liverpool after eight incredible years, during which he became a true club legend. Firmino played an indispensable role throughout his tenure, showcasing selflessness and unmatched energy on the field. His contributions were instrumental in Liverpool's success across various competitions. It was fitting that Firmino found the back of the net at the Kop end, symbolising his deep connection with the fans. Positioned in the centre of the penalty area, Firmino latched onto a through ball from Salah. Although his first touch seemed to take him too wide, Firmino swiftly turned and unleashed a shot, catching De Gea off guard. Diogo Dalot attempted to clear the ball off the line but was unsuccessful, solidifying the humiliation of Manchester United.

As mentioned, the outcome of the match was beyond anyone's expectations. Despite scoring seven goals, it was still only three points, three points that at the time felt like a step in the right direction. Following the best game and performance of the season, Liverpool couldn't allow complacency to set in. However, after one of the highest highs of the season came one of the lowest lows.

Bournemouth 1 - 0 Liverpool

Premier League
Saturday, 11th March 2023
Vitality Stadium

This disappointing result against bottom-of-the-table Bournemouth summed up Liverpool's season perfectly. One step forward and two steps back. We all wondered how Liverpool beat can Manchester United so emphatically six days earlier and then lost to Bournemouth. It was one extreme to the other, the absolute definition of our emotional rollercoaster season.

Liverpool's performance was lacklustre, sluggish, devoid of energy, and detrimental to the team's confidence. Similar to other subpar displays this season, there was a notable absence of standout performers within the Liverpool team. Even players who are typically a source of inspiration, such as Virgil Van Dijk and Mohamed Salah, had an off day, delivering performances among their poorest of the season–a significant statement given the team's struggles. As the captain, Virgil's underwhelming and frustrating performance fell short of the expectations placed upon a leader. If Jordan Henderson had performed similarly, it would have undoubtedly evoked strong reactions and prompted discussions about his captaincy. .

A few weeks earlier, Virgil mentioned that the team's underwhelming performances this season had been attributed to physical and mental fatigue. However, it was clear that Virgil's disappointing display against Bournemouth cannot be solely attributed to exhaustion. It appeared to be a lack of motivation on his part. To be candid, as an exceptional defender, Virgil should have outshone the opposition's players. In this match, though, he seemed disinterested and devoid of his usual drive. There was a moment where Dominic Solanke ran past Virgil and played a ball to Dango Ouattara to create a good chance for Bournemouth. They didn't score from this attack, but it showed what Bournemouth was capable of, and Liverpool should have taken note.

During the build-up for Bournemouth's goal, Virgil demonstrated a lack of determination to win the ball from Ouattara. He allowed Ouattara to bypass him, dribbling deeper into the penalty area. Virgil seemed indifferent, merely observing as Ouattara executed a short pass across the box for Philip Billing to score. It was a goal that could have been prevented if there with a stronger mentality on the field. Ibrahima Konaté tried to intercept the cross, stretching to reach it, but unfortunately, he couldn't make contact, leaving Billing with an easy side-foot finish. Virgil's subsequent gesture of frustration, raising his arms in disappointment, did little to absolve him of the responsibility for this goal.

Diogo Jota's introduction at halftime brought a much-needed spark to Liverpool's performance. His energetic display and attacking intent made an immediate impact. Jota's first shot on goal forced a good save from the Bournemouth goalkeeper, showcasing his threat in front of goal. Later, Jota had a header which led to a crucial moment in the match. His goal attempt was handled by Bournemouth defender Adam Smith, who had his arm in an unnatural position, denying a clear goal-scoring opportunity. Initially, the referee signalled for a corner, but after a VAR review, the decision was rightly overturned, and Liverpool were awarded a penalty. This intervention by VAR ensured the correct outcome and gave Liverpool a chance to get back into the game.

Mohamed Salah's penalty miss was undoubtedly a significant moment in the match and reflected his overall performance against Bournemouth. It starkly contrasted his exceptional display against Manchester United just six days prior. Salah seemed to struggle and couldn't reproduce the same level of impact in this game. Examining Salah's match statistics, it's clear that his output fell below his usual standards. Salah had two shots but only had one on target from open play. The other shot was from his penalty miss. Salah had a pass accuracy of 76.7% with twenty-three accurate passes, and he had no key passes or accurate crosses. He won one of his four ground duels and lost possession fourteen times. It was a tough afternoon for Salah and all supporters to witness.

Liverpool's loss against Bournemouth was undoubtedly a setback, even more so considering their recent victories. It highlighted the inconsistency that Liverpool had struggled with all season. Liverpool couldn't score a goal against the team with the worst defence in the league (at the time of playing), and with the second leg against Real Madrid looming, things didn't look good. All I asked from the match at the Bernabéu was not to get humiliated.

Real Madrid 1 - 0 Liverpool
(6 - 2) Agg.

UEFA Champions League R-16, Second Leg
Wednesday, 15th March 2023
Santiago Bernabéu Stadium

As expected, Liverpool's journey in the Champions League ended with a 1-0 defeat against Real Madrid in the second leg. While a 1-0 loss to a formidable opponent like Real Madrid is not necessarily embarrassing, it was still disappointing. It seems that Liverpool met the challenge I set for them to avoid humiliation at the Bernabéu. They managed to put up a resilient performance and kept the scoreline close.

It would always be challenging to overturn the 5-2 deficit from the first leg against a potent Real Madrid side. Considering Liverpool's inconsistent form throughout the season, the likelihood of a comeback seemed even more unlikely. In his pre-match press conference, Jürgen Klopp's statement that Liverpool had a 1% chance of advancing to the quarter-finals reflected the daunting nature of the task. While the remark might have been seen as an admission of the enormity of the challenge, it was also a realistic assessment of the situation.

The absence of Jordan Henderson due to illness and Stefan Bajčetić's injury added to Liverpool's challenges ahead of the match against Real Madrid. As the team's captain, Henderson brings leadership and experience. His absence limited Liverpool's midfield options. Additionally, the news of Bajčetić's injury and his confirmation on social media that he would miss the rest of the season further impacted Liverpool's midfield concerns.

Klopp opted for a two-player double pivot with Fabinho and James Milner in midfield while fielding an additional attacking player to compensate for the absence of a midfielder. Klopp chose to alter the formation instead of starting players like Harvey Elliott, Alex Oxlade-Chamberlain, Curtis Jones, or Naby Keïta. Keïta, who had a disastrous performance against Crystal Palace, had not featured for Liverpool since. Real Madrid's midfield trio of Eduardo Camavinga, Toni Kroos, and Luka Modrić understandably dominated the midfield battle.

Liverpool's performance was flat, failing to generate clear-cut chances that would trouble Real Madrid throughout the match. Although Darwin Núñez created an opportunity by beating Real Madrid's right-back and forcing Thibaut Courtois to make a save, it was an isolated moment in an otherwise unimpressive attacking display. The xG (expected goals) statistic, which measures the quality of scoring opportunities, further emphasised Liverpool's lack of meaningful chances. An xG of 0.52 highlighted the slim probability of Liverpool scoring, let alone achieving the three goals required to level the aggregate score. It was clear that Liverpool would have been fortunate to find the back of the net once, given their limited scoring opportunities.

To add to the frustrations, the goal Liverpool conceded in the Bernabéu was disappointing. The sequence leading up to the goal showed more defensive lapses and a lack of coordination. With Liverpool positioning themselves defensively, Camavinga played a pass from deep to Karim Benzema, who found himself between Virgil van Dijk and Ibrahima Konaté. As Benzema received the pass, Virgil attempted a challenge, while Konaté seemed uncertain about how to position himself. The French defender tried to move in front of Benzema to intercept the pass, but this took him out of the equation. Virgil's tackle resulted in the ball falling to Vinícius Júnior, who tried to shoot but missed and fell. While on the ground, Vinícius passed it across to Benzema for a straightforward tap-in. Konaté failed to drop back and mark Benzema, allowing him to score easily.

During a call-in show on the Team Kopish YouTube channel, a caller made a thought-provoking statement about Liverpool's injury issues. The caller suggested that it is not the individual players who are injury-prone but the system in place that is prone to injuries. This observation is supported by the fact that Liverpool experienced more injuries than other teams in the Premier League this season.

It is widely known that Liverpool trains with the same intensity during their training sessions as they would during actual matches. This level of intensity has been a defining characteristic of the team's success in previous seasons. However, it raises the question of whether maintaining such high training intensity is necessary or if it contributes to the team's injury woes.

While adjusting the training intensity may be a potential solution, it is vital to consider the potential impact on Liverpool's playing style and overall team dynamics. The high-intensity training sessions have been a critical factor that sets Liverpool apart from other teams. It has helped them achieve success in the past, so it is a tough decision. Blaming the medical department alone would be unfair, as addressing the injury-prone system requires a collective effort. Liverpool must carefully evaluate their training methods and collaborate with the medical staff to balance their fitness levels and minimise the risk of injuries. Finding the right approach will be essential to ensure that their world-class players can consistently contribute on the pitch rather than missing significant portions of the season due to injury.

The injury records of players such as Thiago, Naby Keïta, and Joël Matip, to name a few, raise valid concerns about Liverpool's ongoing struggles with injuries. According to statistics from transfermarket.co.uk, Thiago has missed sixty-six games during his time at Liverpool, although three of those matches were due to Covid. Naby Keïta has missed one hundred and five games in his almost six-year tenure, while Joël Matip has missed one hundred and three games after nearly seven years at the club.

These numbers highlight the pressing need for improvement in this area. Liverpool should be able to rely on the availability and fitness of these players throughout the season to utilise the squad entirely. By striving to reduce the frequency and severity of injuries, Liverpool can enhance their squad depth and consistently increase their chances of success. This would need collaborative efforts from the club's medical staff, coaching team, sports science department, and players to ensure better availability and sustained impact on the team.

Mohamed Salah's relatively low injury record at Liverpool, with only three matches missed (one due to Covid), highlights the importance of optimising *every* aspect of the club's operations, both on and off the pitch. To truly evolve, Liverpool must prioritise availability in recruitment but also elite-level backroom staff. The club must invest in elite physiotherapists, sports scientists, data analysts, fitness coaches, conditioning specialists, and recovery coaches.

This comprehensive approach is crucial in the modern era, particularly for a club like Liverpool, which uses data to gain advantages. These changes are necessary to address the injury concerns and ensure the long-term success and performance of the team. By bolstering their backroom staff and implementing cutting-edge practices, Liverpool can strive for optimal player fitness, reduced injury frequency, and ultimately unlock the squad's full potential.

So Liverpool was out of the Champions League, which was to be expected after the first leg's result. It was now top four or bust.

April
2023

- Manchester City (A) - 1st April - EPL - Page 294

- Chelsea (A) - 4th April - EPL - Page 302

- Arsenal (H) - 9th April - EPL - Page 306

- Leeds Utd. (A) - 17th April - EPL - Page 313

- Nottm. Forest (H) - 22nd April - EPL - Page 306

- West Ham (A) - 26th April - EPL - Page 327

- Tottenham (H) - 30th April - EPL - Page 332

Manchester City 4 - 1 Liverpool

Premier League
Saturday, 1st April 2023
Etihad Stadium

After a lengthy break, the team could not gain momentum and struggled to assert themselves in this match. The first half may have shown some promise, but a significant drop-off in the second half led to a disappointing result. The contrasting performances between the two halves further highlighted the need for better in-game management and consistency.

The contrast between Liverpool's first and second-half performances against Manchester City was stark. In the initial forty-five minutes, Liverpool executed their game plan effectively, staying solid defensively and posing a threat on the counter-attack. However, the same cannot be said for the second half. The team seemed to lose momentum and struggled to maintain their earlier intensity. Manchester City took control of the match and dominated proceedings, leading to a one-sided affair. The attacking momentum graph for this match clearly illustrates City's growing dominance as the game progressed. Liverpool's lack of effort and desire in the second half was disappointing but clear.

Despite Manchester City's dominance, Liverpool managed to open the scoring by executing their game plan well. The goal came from a quick transition and a well-timed pass from Trent Alexander-Arnold to Diogo Jota, who was positioned on the shoulder of the last defender, helped by City's high defensive line. Jota did well to hold off a defender and create an opportunity for Mohamed Salah, who was in the right place to collect the loose ball. Salah showed composure and skill as he struck the ball with his left foot, finding the back of the net and giving Liverpool the lead. However, the positive momentum didn't last, and Liverpool's performance deteriorated.

Manchester City's wide attacking players, Riyad Mahrez and Jack Grealish, were causing problems for Liverpool's full-backs, Andy Robertson and Trent Alexander-Arnold. The lack of midfield protection left Robertson and Trent in vulnerable one-on-one situations, allowing City to exploit the space and create scoring opportunities. City's equaliser came as a result of their effective combination play. Mahrez was able to outmanoeuvre Robertson and find İlkay Gündoğan in a central position. Gündoğan, with excellent control, passed the ball out wide to Grealish, who swiftly delivered a cross back into the box. Julián Álvarez capitalised on the chance with a composed sidefoot finish, levelling the score. It was a well-executed goal that showcased City's attacking ability. From then on, Manchester City gained more confidence and continued asserting their dominance in the game. They built upon their equaliser and grew stronger as the match progressed.

Upon closer analysis of Manchester City's first goal, it became clear that there were defensive lapses from Virgil van Dijk and Ibrahima Konaté that allowed City to exploit the gaps in Liverpool's defence. As Riyad Mahrez moved infield, Virgil followed him, leaving a significant gap at the back that took him out of the play. This left the defensive line vulnerable and created space for City to exploit. When İlkay Gündoğan received the pass from Mahrez, Konaté attempted to intercept the pass but was unsuccessful, leaving the ball to reach its intended target. This missed interception further exposed Liverpool's defence and allowed City to progress their attack. As the ball was played out wide to Jack Grealish, both central defenders, Virgil and Konaté, found themselves outside the box, unable to influence the play. Trent

Alexander-Arnold could not block the Grealish cross, and Jordan Henderson, who was filling in the gap at the centre-back position, couldn't get close enough to Julián Álvarez to prevent the goal. The combination of Virgil moving inside with Mahrez and Konaté missing the interception created a situation where both defenders were out of position, making it easier for Manchester City to score. Another sequence of defensive errors and poor positioning allowed City to take advantage and find the back of the net.

The goal that gave Manchester City the lead exposed *more* defensive shortcomings in Liverpool's backline. The sequence of events highlighted the lack of coordination within the defence. At the start of the second half, Trent Alexander-Arnold decided to press the ball, leaving a substantial gap in the right-back position. Ibrahima Konaté recognised the gap and shifted over to cover, while Virgil van Dijk followed and occupied the space vacated by Konaté. This left a noticeable void where Virgil would typically be positioned in a typical defensive setup.

Andy Robertson couldn't shift across to cover the space like the other defenders because Mahrez occupied him on the wing. With Liverpool's defensive structure compromised, Julián Álvarez played a cross-field pass just inside Liverpool's half, finding Mahrez. As Mahrez received the pass, Kevin De Bruyne made a central run into the box, exploiting the hole in Liverpool's defence. Virgil attempted to chase back and regain a goalside position on De Bruyne, but he could not do so. It's worth noting that De Bruyne was initially in an offside position when the pass was played to Mahrez, meaning he had a head start and an advantage. Mahrez played the ball across the box to De Bruyne, who lunged and hit the ball into the back of the net.

Manchester City capitalised on the defensive gaps and made it look effortless due to the generous space and lack of organisation in Liverpool's defence. The defensive errors, including Trent pressing the ball alone and leaving a gap, gave City an advantage they expertly exploited. When facing a dangerous team like Manchester City, such defensive mistakes will be costly and result in goals.

The goal signalled a shift in momentum, as Manchester City sensed an opportunity to take advantage of Liverpool's vulnerability. They were determined to exploit the situation and further extend their lead. Liverpool appeared susceptible and vulnerable, providing City with the confidence and belief that they could dominate and win the match. The goal conceded early in the second half exposed Liverpool's fragility and made it apparent that they were there for the taking. With heads dropping and confidence shattered, Liverpool's primary objective shifted to damage limitation, attempting to prevent further goals and limit the damage inflicted by Manchester City's relentless attacking play. In this critical phase of the match, Liverpool found themselves on the back foot, struggling to keep composure and mount a meaningful response.

Even with Liverpool trying to be compact defensively, Manchester City proved their ability to unlock tight defences and create more scoring opportunities. Despite Liverpool's two lines of four, City's ability to find pockets of space combined with their fluid ball movement posed significant challenges for the Reds. Riyad Mahrez's penetrating dribble into the box from a wide area caused immediate problems for Liverpool's defence. Despite Andy Robertson and Jordan Henderson attempting to close him down, they could not make a decisive challenge, allowing Mahrez to pick out Julián Álvarez in the penalty area. Álvarez unleashed a shot that Trent Alexander-Arnold blocked, but the loose ball fell kindly to İlkay Gündoğan. With enough time and space, Gündoğan took a touch and expertly lifted the ball into the back of the net.

Manchester City's fourth and final goal was scored by Jack Grealish, who had an exceptional performance in a Manchester City shirt. The goal was a result of a well-executed attacking move by City. İlkay Gündoğan initiated the play with a cross-field pass to find Jack Grealish on the left wing. Meanwhile, Kevin de Bruyne made a clever run behind Trent Alexander-Arnold. Grealish received the ball and played it down the line, continuing his run into the penalty box. De Bruyne returned the pass to Grealish, who confidently struck the ball into the net.

The goal put City in a commanding position, and it was a challenging situation for Trent Alexander-Arnold, who found himself isolated after the cross-field pass, with Grealish and De Bruyne combining around him effectively. However, it must be noted that Trent's failure to track Grealish's run into the box after he played the pass down the line left room for criticism.

In his post-match press conference, Jürgen Klopp took a different approach by openly addressing the team's performance and not shying away from criticising certain players' and their motivation levels. Rather than diverting attention or making excuses, Klopp held the players accountable for their poor showing. This approach was seen as a departure from his usual stance of protecting the players in public and taking the blame upon himself. By calling out the players, Klopp may have wanted to emphasise the need for improvement and highlight areas where individual performances fell short. Holding players accountable sometimes serves as a wake-up call and motivates them to raise their standards. Klopp said:

The two midfielders, Hendo and Fab, worked a lot and tried to close gaps. Cody [Gakpo] worked a lot, especially in possession, tried to close gaps, and Alisson, of course. If you want to get something from here, fourteen or fifteen players have to be on top of their game, and that was not the case.

The season felt like it was over following this defeat to City. However, the unpredictable nature of football often surprises us. Liverpool remained undefeated from this point until the end of the season. Klopp's post-match comments had the desired effect and ignited a fire within the players, leading to a remarkable, almost unbelievable turnaround in form.

Chelsea 0 - 0 Liverpool

Premier League
Tuesday, 4th April 2023
Stamford Bridge

Liverpool played a goalless draw at Stamford Bridge in an uneventful match. Chelsea's attacking line seemed out-of-form and lacked confidence as they failed to convert their chances. In contrast, Liverpool appeared fortunate to secure a point, with luck favouring them on the day. The team's overall performance was subpar once again. Jürgen Klopp's decision to make six changes to the starting lineup raised questions. Whether these changes were in response to recent underwhelming performances, indicating Klopp's frustration and desire for improvement, or if they were made strategically to rest key players ahead of the more challenging upcoming match against Arsenal.

During a pre-match interview with Sky Sports, Klopp clarified his team selection. He explained that Virgil van Dijk could not travel to London due to illness, and the decision to rest other players was based on the need for fresh legs. However, Klopp's comments seemed contradictory when he stated, "We needed fresh legs and fresh minds," and hinted at the opportunity for other players due to the dissatisfaction with recent performances.

Understanding Klopp's true intentions behind the squad rotation remained a challenge. However, it was clear that a change *was* needed, given the underwhelming performances thus far. Klopp acknowledged the importance of providing an opportunity for squad players to prove themselves in the first team, as their inclusion couldn't possibly result in a worse outcome than what had been witnessed previously.

Chelsea's two disallowed goals provided a sense of relief for Liverpool, as both instances were accurately overturned. The first goal was denied due to Reece James being marginally offside, while the second was rightfully ruled out because Kai Havertz's shot deflected off his arm into the net after an initial save by Alisson. The presence of VAR played a crucial role in preventing Chelsea from adding to Liverpool's troubles.

Jordan Henderson displayed visible frustration during the match, expressing his discontent by arguing and raising his voice towards his teammates. While his intentions may have been to motivate the team, his actions were not universally well-received. Some fans believed Henderson should focus on *his* performance, while others appreciated his efforts to rally and push the team forward. However, it is widely agreed that Henderson crossed a line when he directed some of his complaints towards Alisson, which was deemed unnecessary.

In the lead-up to this incident, Kalidou Koulibaly delivered a long ball forward for Chelsea, leading to Joël Matip's attempt to clear it with a header. Unfortunately, Matip's clearance was unsuccessful, and the ball ended up with João Félix, who subsequently shot over the bar. Following the incident, Jordan Henderson confronted Alisson, questioning why he didn't tell Matip to leave the ball for the goalkeeper to collect and halt the attack.

It appeared that Alisson was attempting to explain to Henderson that he *did* give the instruction, but Matip did not listen. While no goal resulted from the situation, it wasn't a critical moment that determined the match's outcome. Nevertheless, if there is one player who deserves exemption from the widespread criticism this season, it is Alisson, considering his overall performance and contributions to the team.

Alisson demonstrated his composure and professionalism by addressing the situation and resolving any potential issues between himself and Jordan Henderson while speaking to the sports network ESPN Brazil:

Me and Henderson, we are two people who fight, who give our lives for their team, and on the field, there is no way to ask 'please?'. So sometimes it seems that the mood is high, but it's two people trying to fix it and do things in the best way for the team and try to help.

Respect goes to Alisson for his admirable approach to diffusing the situation and defusing any animosity between himself and Henderson.

It was frustrating to see Liverpool's lack of cutting-edge in the final third and their struggles to find form. While it's understandable that changes were needed after a poor performance, the inconsistency in the lineup may not have aided their efforts to regain momentum and win the match.

Liverpool 2 - 2 Arsenal

Premier League
Sunday, 9th April 2023
Anfield

Jürgen Klopp's pre-match interview, where he accepted sole responsibility for Liverpool's poor form this season, was a bold move that shows his character and leadership. However, it proved my theory wrong. After the loss to Manchester City, I felt like Klopp was no longer protecting the players from the media and supporter criticism. Klopp shouldering the sole responsibility for Liverpool's poor season proved he was still a shield for the players. It made me rethink the situation. I adore Jürgen Klopp, he has been my favourite Liverpool manager during my lifetime, and while I accept he isn't blameless, I'm confident enough to say he isn't the sole contributor to Liverpool's downfall.

The match at Anfield between Liverpool and Arsenal was important for both teams. Arsenal, aiming for a change in fortunes at Anfield, were eager to secure three points as they pursued their dreams of winning their first league title in twenty years. Having spent most of the season at the top of the Premier League, Arsenal entered the match in a strong position. On the contrary, Liverpool had faced difficulties maintaining their form throughout the season, making the game crucial for their aim of a top-four finish.

In the first half, Arsenal had a solid performance and took a 2-0 lead. Liverpool *again* found themselves on the receiving end, facing a team with more aggression and desire. The opening goal came through a clever play by Bukayo Saka, who made an inverted run from the wing to receive a pass. This caused Andy Robertson, the Liverpool full-back, to lose a few yards as he anticipated Saka running down the wing.

Saka received the ball and advanced towards Liverpool's goal, attempting a one-two pass with Martin Ødegaard. However, the return pass inadvertently struck Virgil van Dijk, who could not quickly readjust his footing and clear the ball effectively. As a result, the loose ball fell to Gabriel Martinelli, who skillfully manoeuvred deeper into the box and delicately placed a shot past Alisson, putting Arsenal in the lead. Liverpool's defensive lapse once again proved costly and could have been prevented with more solid defending. Arsenal had taken the lead within eight minutes.

For Arsenal's second goal, Gabriel Martinelli showed his dribbling skills again as he advanced up the left wing. With time and space, he delivered a perfectly curled cross into the box for Gabriel Jesus, who executed a well-placed header to find the back of the net. It was another impressive goal from Arsenal and added more frustration for Liverpool.

In the match, Liverpool's defensive approach had a notable tactical change. This was the first match that saw Trent Alexander-Arnold play the inverted fullback role. Ibrahima Konaté was tasked with covering the right-back position. Trent operated in a defensive midfield area, occasionally dropping back to the centre-back position when Konaté moved out wide to cover. This tactical adjustment allowed Trent to contribute to the team's build-up play from deeper positions as a deep-lying playmaker and reinvigorated his and Liverpool's season.

This inverted fullback role, which uses a full back in a more central midfield area, has regained popularity, with Manchester City utilising it effectively. In a recent match against Liverpool, John Stones had the freedom to roam and often ventured into midfield areas, providing additional support and creating numerical advantages in essential areas. Klopp may have drawn inspiration from Pep Guardiola's tactical approach, incorporating elements of it into Liverpool's game plan. As good as John Stones is in the role, it is a position that looks tailor-made for Trent, who grew in his new role for the remainder of the season.

At this stage of the match, Liverpool had struggled to make an impact in attack, with Arsenal gaining the upper hand in individual battles as the atmosphere at Anfield became subdued. However, a confrontation between Trent Alexander-Arnold and Granit Xhaka sparked a resurgence in the crowd's energy and engagement. The aggressive reaction from the Anfield crowd, voicing their support for Liverpool and expressing their discontent towards the opposition, injected a renewed sense of passion and intensity into the atmosphere. There is a unique power in a passionate Anfield crowd, known for their ability to rally behind the team and create a hostile environment for the opposition. The vocal displays of support amplify the team's spirit and can influence the outcome of a match. Xhaka's actions inadvertently ignited the crowd, awakening their fighting spirit and determination to back their team.

With the crowd reinvigorated, Liverpool began to create scoring opportunities and pulled a goal back just before halftime. The connection between the fans and the players proved to be a lethal combination once more. Curtis Jones, who retained his place in the starting lineup following his energetic display against Chelsea, operated on the left wing during a threatening, offensive move. Jones showed reasonable ball control, holding it up until Diogo Jota ran past him. Jones then released the ball to Jota, who delivered a well-placed cross into the box. In a lunged attempt to reach the ball, Jordan Henderson inadvertently played a pass to the back post, where Mohamed Salah seized the opportunity and scored a crucial tap-in goal. That goal altered the halftime team talks for both sides.

Liverpool's second-half dominance was remarkable, evoking memories of their triumphant campaigns when winning the Champions League and Premier League. The level of dominance they showed was both awe-inspiring and frustrating. It begged why such performances had been so elusive throughout the season or even in the initial thirty minutes of this match. Arsenal found themselves unable to contend with Liverpool's relentless onslaught in the second half, which was a testament to Liverpool's determination. They should have emerged as the victors.

In the fifty-fourth minute, Liverpool was awarded a penalty after Ben White fouled Diogo Jota in the box. Jota cleverly positioned himself between the ball and White, causing the Arsenal defender to catch Jota on the calf clumsily. As VAR reviewed the incident, Trent Alexander-Arnold guarded the penalty spot to prevent any tampering by Arsenal players. At the same time, Jordan Henderson held the ball, initially hinting that he might take the spot kick. After VAR confirmed the penalty, Henderson gave the ball to Mohamed Salah, who unfortunately missed the target with his penalty kick, resulting in a huge missed opportunity for Liverpool. Despite the disappointment of not converting the penalty, Liverpool continued to apply pressure on Arsenal's defence.

In the eighty-seventh minute, Liverpool managed to equalise. Trent Alexander-Arnold showed skill on the right wing, nutmegging Oleksandr Zinchenko before delivering a lofted cross to the back post. Roberto Firmino rose high and directed a header into the net to level the score. There was still enough time left in the match to find a winning goal.

Following the equaliser, Liverpool had several opportunities to secure a victory. Darwin Núñez missed a one-on-one chance against Arsenal goalkeeper Aaron Ramsdale after a delightful through ball from Mohamed Salah. Ramsdale then made a crucial save to deny Salah's curled shot destined for the top corner. In the match's dying moments, Ramsdale kept out a chested effort from Ibrahima Konaté, preventing the ball from crossing the goal line and stopping any potential goal-line scramble. It would have been wiser for Konaté to use his head instead of trying to fumble the ball over the line with his chest, but in fairness, it was instinctual, and Konaté didn't have much time to react to the opportunity. Ramsdale's contributions were vital in preserving the draw for Arsenal.

Despite a disappointing first half, where Liverpool conceded two goals, it was a welcome surprise to witness the improved performance in the second half. While Liverpool could not secure a victory, earning a draw from a 2-0 deficit was commendable. Liverpool had struggled to find their form throughout the season, making it a refreshing change to witness an engaging and entertaining game. With the team's top-four ambitions seemingly no longer feasible, the focus could shift to enjoying the remaining matches and recapturing the joy of watching Liverpool play. As fans, the entertainment factor became more significant without high-stakes competition.

Leeds Utd. 1 - 6 Liverpool

Premier League
Monday, 17th April 2023
Elland Road

Jürgen Klopp described this match as a revenge mission after Leeds' victory at Anfield earlier in the season. Despite the challenging atmosphere at Elland Road, Liverpool showed their dominance throughout the match. Initially, it appeared it could be a tough night, considering Leeds' position in a relegation battle and the passionate support from their fans. However, Liverpool quickly settled into the game and displayed their ruthless attacking talent. Considering Leeds' lacklustre performance, Liverpool found the back of the net six times, securing an emphatic victory.

Trent Alexander-Arnold excelled in his role as an inverted fullback once again. This tactical adjustment allowed him to show his creativity in midfield while still contributing defensively. Initial concerns among fans about his effectiveness in this position were proven wrong as he demonstrated his ability to be a valuable asset in that area of the pitch. In the match, Trent's involvement was significant, with 153 touches and an impressive passing accuracy of 91%. He displayed his playmaking skills by creating two big chances and providing two key passes, resulting in two assists. The positive reception from fans and even football personalities like Gary Lineker, who expressed his desire to see Trent in midfield more often, further emphasised his impact in the role. It would be exciting to witness Trent's continued growth and influence, establishing himself as an even more formidable threat in the seasons to come with further experience and maturity in this new position.

Liverpool opened the scoring in the thirty-fifth minute with a well-executed team goal. Trent Alexander-Arnold played a pivotal role in the build-up, winning the ball in midfield before making an overlapping run to receive a pass from Mohamed Salah. Trent then delivered a composed low cross across the box, allowing Cody Gakpo to tap the ball into the net. It was an impressive display of Trent's ability to contribute to both midfield and the attacking third. However, there was some controversy surrounding the goal as replays revealed that the initial challenge by Trent involved the ball striking his arm. VAR determined that the incident occurred far enough back in the build-up and did not directly influence the goal, which led to understandable frustrations from the Leeds fans and players.

Liverpool extended their lead just before halftime with another well-crafted goal. Diogo Jota showed his ball-winning ability in midfield and demonstrated great composure as he dribbled forward. He then provided a precise pass to Mohamed Salah, who displayed his intelligent movement by making a clever run from the right wing to the left, confusing the Leeds defence. Salah expertly allowed the ball to roll in front of him, enabling him to unleash a powerful high shot at the near post, which goalkeeper Illan Meslier couldn't prevent from finding the back of the net. Scoring a second goal away from home before halftime was a rare occurrence for Liverpool this season, and it provided them with a significant advantage going into the break.

In the early stages of the second half, an error from Ibrahima Konaté allowed Leeds to get back into the match. After Salah passed the ball back to the centre-back, two Leeds players pressed him, and one of the pressing players, Luis Sinisterra, successfully tackled Konaté, allowing him to break through on goal with no other defensive cover. Sinisterra showed composure by chipping the ball over Alisson, who had rushed out to close down the angle, resulting in a goal for

Leeds. At this critical moment, the game could have taken a different turn. Liverpool could have succumbed to the pressure, conceded another goal, and experienced the frustration of losing a two-goal lead. However, despite witnessing similar scenarios unfold multiple times this season, Liverpool didn't crumble. Instead, they responded with determination and resilience. They shifted the momentum back in their favour, scoring four more goals and seizing control of the match.

Liverpool extended their lead just five minutes after Leeds had pulled a goal back, and it was a goal that would have made throw-in coach Thomas Grønnemark proud. It all started with Trent taking a throw-in from the right-back position. The ball reached Curtis Jones in midfield, who showed his vision and skill by delivering a sublime, curled through-ball pass to Diogo Jota. Seizing the opportunity, Jota struck the ball with a first-time shot from the edge of the box, expertly guiding it around and over Meslier. It was a stunning finish, made even more impressive by the pass quality that set it up. This goal was a testament to the abilities of both Jones and Jota, with the latter breaking his scoring drought of over a year in style.

In May 2022, it was announced that Liverpool and Thomas Grønnemark would be parting ways after a successful five-year working relationship. Grønnemark, the renowned throw-in specialist, significantly impacted Liverpool's performance in throw-ins under pressure, elevating them from 18th to 1st in the Premier League rankings. When Liverpool initially appointed Grønnemark, there were sceptics and critics, including figures like Richard Keys, Andy Gray, and Steve Nicol, who dismissed hiring a throw-in coach as "absolute nonsense." However, the results speak for themselves, and Grønnemark's influence on the team's ball retention and overall improvement cannot be denied. The departure of the Danish specialist was met with the club's well wishes, acknowledging the valuable contributions he made during his time with the club.

Liverpool's fourth goal was a fantastic display of counter-attacking football, reminiscent of the team's style in the past. The sequence started with Andy Robertson winning the ball back at the edge of Liverpool's box. He was also the player that played a well-placed pass that travelled across the Leeds box. Cody Gakpo, who received the ball amidst pressure from several Leeds players, remained composed and decided to pass it to the open Mohamed Salah on his right. Salah demonstrated composure as he controlled the ball and expertly lifted it past the Leeds goalkeeper. The goal demonstrated Liverpool's ability to execute quick, incisive attacks, leaving the Leeds defenders scrambling to stop the shot. With four goals already scored at Elland Road, Liverpool had firmly established their dominance in the match.

Liverpool's fifth goal showcased the bravery and persistence of Diogo Jota. Jordan Henderson provided an accurate cross-cum-pass, finding Jota, who was positioned at the edge of the box. Despite the ball being slightly miss-hit off his shin, Jota hit a half-volleyed shot that struck the inside of the post, eluding the reach of Leeds' goalkeeper. While the goal may have had an element of luck, Jota's confidence due to his earlier goal allowed him to take the shot and see what unfolded. This display of faith resulted in Jota ending the match with two goals and an assist, contributing significantly to Liverpool's convincing performance. It was now crucial for Jota to maintain his fitness and play with freedom until the end of the season, having overcome the pressure of not finding the back of the net.

Liverpool continued their attack with yet another goal. Trent Alexander-Arnold showed excellent vision and precision with a lofted through ball to substitute Darwin

Núñez, who demonstrated perfect timing in his run. Núñez controlled the ball with his chest, took a composed touch with his left foot to set himself up, and then confidently struck the ball into the back of the net, sealing the match's final goal. Trent's contribution *again* emphasised his significance to the Liverpool team, particularly in a central role where he can utilise his passing ability and influence the team's possession game.

After the match, Jamie Carragher praised Trent's outstanding performance. According to Carragher, the only player in the league who can surpass Trent in splitting defences with a single pass is Manchester City's Kevin De Bruyne. This new role that Trent had been given is ideally suited to his strengths, and Carragher believes it should be the future evolution of Liverpool Football Club, something I can get behind.

In the end, Liverpool secured a comfortable victory, which was truly satisfying. Despite an error from Konaté, the overall performance from the Reds was exceptional and ruthless, particularly considering it was an away game. There was undoubtedly a sense of rejuvenation within the team, with the experimentation of Trent in an inverted fullback role and the team playing a fluid and expressive style of football. As fans, we had endured a challenging season, making it all the more refreshing and enjoyable to witness Liverpool's captivating football again.

Additionally, it is worth noting that Luis Díaz returned triumphantly to action following a lengthy injury layoff. While it may have been unrealistic to expect him to immediately show his full potential in the few matches remaining, it was a joyous sight to witness him back on the pitch.

Liverpool 3 - 2 Nottm. Forest

Premier League
Saturday, 22nd April 2023
Anfield

Confidence is a peculiar and powerful element in life and football. Diogo Jota's goal drought spanning a calendar year can be attributed, in part, to his limited playing time due to multiple injuries. However, his recent performance, with two goals against Leeds and another two against Nottingham Forest, has seemingly sparked a resurgence in his form and ability to influence matches.

The same principle of confidence can be applied to the collective team. Liverpool's struggles this season, marked by poor results and frequently conceding first, can be attributed to a lack of confidence that has permeated the squad. A team's lack of confidence can considerably impact their performance and results. Confidence plays a pivotal role in football, affecting decision-making, belief, and the ability to perform at an elite level. When a team is confident, players can exhibit greater freedom, creativity, and effectiveness on the field.

Following the idea of the match against Leeds being a revenge mission, a similar sentiment could be applied to Liverpool's game against Nottingham Forest. In their previous encounter earlier in the season, Liverpool suffered a defeat in what was considered one of their weakest performances of the campaign. It's reasonable to assume that Liverpool would have been motivated to secure a victory in this match, seeking to avenge their loss from the reverse fixture. The first half of the game was forgettable. However, the match came alive and gained momentum during the second half, providing excitement and intensity.

In the second half's early stages, Liverpool broke the deadlock. It all started with a corner kick taken by Trent Alexander-Arnold, which unintentionally struck Forest defender Moussa Niakhaté. The deflection worked in Liverpool's favour as the ball reached Fabinho, who headed it towards the goal. Despite the likelihood of a covering Forest defender clearing his header off the line, Fabinho appeared unfazed when Diogo Jota finished the ball from close range, about a yard out. Fabinho celebrated alongside Jota, and there was no animosity.

Shortly after, Nottingham Forest managed to equalise. Neco Williams, the former Liverpool player, struck a shot from outside the box, which unfortunately deflected off Andy Robertson. This deflection altered the ball's trajectory and caught Alisson off guard, leaving him wrong-footed. Despite Alisson's effort to get a hand on the ball, it still had too much power and found its way into the net. It wasn't very reassuring to witness Forest quickly level the score, but the deflection introduced an element of luck.

Liverpool regained the lead through an exceptional goal by Diogo Jota. The opportunity arose from a wide set piece taken by Andy Robertson from the left side of the pitch. Nottingham Forest's defensive organisation could have been better, leaving Jota ample time and space in the penalty area. Jota demonstrated remarkable skill and composure as he controlled the incoming ball with his chest, expertly used his knee to prevent it from dropping, and swiftly executed a swivel and volley motion. The strike found the bottom corner of the net, leaving Forest goalkeeper Keylor Navas helpless and unable to make a save. It was an exquisite display of Jota's technique, highlighting his growing confidence with each passing game.

Nottingham Forest employed a long throw-in strategy to exploit Liverpool's defence, reminiscent of the tactics used by Stoke City during the Rory Delap era. This approach was not a criticism but rather an acknowledgement of Forest's determination to find an advantage against Liverpool. The long throw-ins proved to be a significant challenge for Liverpool to defend, and it became a recurring theme throughout the match, particularly when Forest pressed for another equaliser.

During one of these long throw-ins, Moussa Niakhaté delivered a long throw into Liverpool's penalty area. Liverpool struggled to defend the second phase of the throw-in, which became a recurring issue as the match progressed. The ball ultimately fell to Morgan Gibbs-White, who struck a low volley towards the Liverpool goal. The shot took two deflections along the way, making any potential save by Alisson more difficult. As a result, Forest successfully pulled the score level once again.

Liverpool's ability to maintain their composure and secure a victory in a situation that may have seen them drop points in previous weeks was a testament to their growth in confidence. Set pieces played a decisive role in the match, with Liverpool capitalising on a wide free kick to extend their lead again. Trent Alexander-Arnold expertly delivered a floated ball into the box from the wing. Mohamed Salah displayed his predatory instincts as he connected with the cross, directing a powerful shot into the bottom corner. Forest goalkeeper Keylor Navas remained stationary, recognising that he had been beaten when Salah made contact with the ball and unleashed his shot. By finding the courage to go on and secure the victory, Liverpool showed their progress and the ability to overcome previous challenges.

Despite securing the third goal, Liverpool's defence continued to face pressure from Nottingham Forest, particularly from the long throws of Moussa Niakhaté. These long throws created several opportunities for Forest, although they could not convert them into goals. During a scramble in the box from a Forest throw, Taiwo Awoniyi attempted a bicycle kick but narrowly sent his effort over the crossbar. Additionally, substitute Brennan Johnson struck the crossbar with a delicate chip over Alisson following yet another thrown ball into Liverpool's penalty area. Liverpool escaped conceding on these occasions, but it highlighted the need for defensive improvement. The defence's performance during these situations was subpar, sometimes resembling a pinball game. Liverpool struggled to clear the ball effectively, allowing the play to develop into the second phase and beyond. Liverpool needs to improve this issue during the summer break.

West Ham 1 - 2 Liverpool

Premier League
Wednesday, 26th April 2023
London Stadium

Call me pessimistic, but I had anticipated that Liverpool would drop points against West Ham. I believed it would be a challenging night for Liverpool, resulting in dropped points. However, I'm glad to say that I was proven wrong. Liverpool displayed great character, coming from behind to secure all three points in London. This victory marked their third consecutive win, extending their unbeaten streak to five matches.

One of the pre-match concerns was the absence of Ibrahima Konaté due to a slight knock. Joël Matip had to step in, potentially affecting Liverpool's defensive performance. The tactical adjustment of Trent Alexander-Arnold playing as an inverted full-back meant that Konaté's role of covering the space at right-back was crucial. However, any worries regarding Matip's ability to fulfil this role were unfounded. Fortunately, Matip returned to the team looking rejuvenated after his time out of the starting lineup. Not only did he excel defensively, but he also emerged as the match-winner, securing the final goal that led to Liverpool's 2-1 victory.

Liverpool began the match positively, maintaining control of the ball and playing with notable intensity. However, it was during West Ham's first dangerous attack that they managed to take the lead. The goal was the result of a well-executed play by West Ham. Lucas Paquetá and Michail Antonio combined with a swift one-two pass at the edge of Liverpool's penalty area, allowing Paquetá to unleash a powerful shot towards the goal. Although the shot was struck with force, there was room for criticism regarding Alisson's positioning. The shot seemed to be directed more towards the centre of the goal rather than the corners, which led to the belief that Alisson could have potentially saved it had he been better positioned.

The shift in mentality within the Liverpool team over the past few weeks has been notable. In previous months, a setback like conceding the first goal would have affected the players' confidence, resulting in a downward spiral and potentially more goals conceded as the team struggled to recover. However, the recent performances have shown a different mindset. One that is a lot more resilient and confident in their ability.

Liverpool responded quickly after conceding with an impressive goal by Cody Gakpo. The pass from Trent Alexander-Arnold in the build-up to Gakpo's goal should not go unnoticed. While it may have appeared like a simple sidefoot pass, its significance lies in its accuracy. Trent's well-executed pass, played precisely between Declan Rice and Tomáš Souček, created a crucial opening for Gakpo to exploit. This perfectly weighted ball that broke West Ham lines allowed Gakpo to receive it with one touch and set himself up for the impressive right-footed strike that found the back of the net. Gakpo's brilliance in finishing the chance cannot be understated either, hitting a low shot from thirty yards that beat Łukasz Fabiański to equalise for the Reds.

For the next several minutes, West Ham seemed determined to hold on while Liverpool continued to create chances. Jota had an opportunity where he narrowly missed the target, shooting just over the bar. Another chance came from a near-post header flicked on by Jordan Henderson, but Jota couldn't make clean contact with the ball, and it ended up on the wrong side of the post. However, West Ham also had moments and came close to scoring too.

In a counter-attacking move, Saïd Benrahma dribbled into the box and played a low cross to Michail Antonio, who was in a perfect position for a simple tap-in goal. But to Liverpool's relief, Virgil Van Dijk managed to get the slightest of touches on the ball, throwing off Antonio's timing, and the ball went out for a West Ham corner. It was a crucial intervention from Virgil, showcasing his defensive prowess and preventing West Ham from regaining the advantage.

The second half saw another tense moment when Jarrod Bowen appeared to have scored for West Ham. However, VAR ruled him offside, ultimately disallowing the goal. It was a fortunate turn of events for Liverpool, as West Ham's potential second goal was ruled out.

Liverpool's winning goal was a result of a well-executed set piece. Andy Robertson delivered an out-swinging corner, perfectly placing the ball into the danger area. Joël Matip displayed excellent timing and positioning as he soared above the West Ham defenders to meet the ball with a powerful header. Matip's connection with the header was superb, generating tremendous power and accuracy. The sheer force behind the shot left little chance for Łukasz Fabiański to make a save.

Late in the match, a moment of controversy involved a potential handball incident. Declan Rice dribbled into the box and attempted to pass the ball to Tomáš Souček, who was caught off guard and failed to meet the pass. Thiago Alcântara, displaying quick reflexes, intercepted the ball and engaged in a tussle with Danny Ings for possession. During the scramble, Thiago slipped and fell, inadvertently making contact with the ball using his hand as he tried to protect himself from the fall.

West Ham players immediately appealed for a penalty, which was understandable, given that the ball struck Thiago's hand. However, according to the handball rules, the situation falls under the category of using the arm to break a fall, which is not considered a handball offence. The decision not to award a penalty sparked strong reactions, mainly from West Ham manager David Moyes, visibly frustrated by the outcome. Regardless, the referee made the right decision as per the rule book.

So Liverpool continued their winning streak with a crucial victory against West Ham in the capital, and at this stage of the season, securing wins was paramount. The team's confidence was growing, building momentum with each successive triumph. It was encouraging to see Liverpool maintain a decent run of form.

Liverpool 4 - 3 Tottenham

Premier League
Sunday, 30th April 2023
Anfield

There had been plenty of memorable moments this season, from thrilling end-to-end encounters that resembled basketball rather than football to matches filled with unexpected twists. However, the game against Tottenham is one of the craziest. Liverpool capitalised on an underwhelming Tottenham side, surging to a commanding three-goal lead early. Yet, in a dramatic turn of events, they let go of their advantage during the game's final moments, making it a truly unpredictable affair. If that wasn't enough, Liverpool grabbed a late winner to send Anfield into euphoric cheer.

Liverpool made an impressive start to the match, taking the lead after just three minutes. The breakthrough came from a fantastic play orchestrated by Trent Alexander-Arnold. He delivered a perfect cross into the box precisely and accurately, finding Curtis Jones in an ideal position. Jones showed composure and skill as he calmly slotted the ball past

Tottenham's goalkeeper, Fraser Forster. Alexander-Arnold's delivery was exquisite, highlighting his impact on the team since adopting the inverted full-back role. He has been influential in Liverpool's recent performances, with six assists in the last five games.

Later, Liverpool extended their lead to 2-0 with a splendid team goal. Mohamed Salah used his vision by playing a well-weighted through ball behind Tottenham's defence. Cody Gakpo displayed excellent awareness and skill as he managed to keep the ball in play and deliver a precise cross into the box. Luis Díaz showed his finishing ability by volleying the ball first-time into the net, beating Fraser Forster at his near post. It was a moment of great emotion for Díaz, who celebrated his goal as a well-deserved reward for his perseverance and determination while recovering from injury.

Liverpool further solidified their lead in the fifteenth minute with a confidently taken penalty by Mohamed Salah. The opportunity arose when Cody Gakpo was clumsily brought down by Tottenham's defender Cristian Romero inside the box. The foul was clear-cut, leaving no room for debate. Despite Romero's protests, Salah calmly stepped up to the spot and dispatched the penalty by placing the ball high and down the middle of the goal, out of the reach of the goalkeeper. The successful conversion made it 3-0 in favour of Liverpool, putting them in a commanding position early in the match.

Liverpool found themselves in a comfortable position with a three-goal lead, seemingly putting the match out of reach for Tottenham. At that moment, it appeared unlikely that Tottenham could mount a comeback. The atmosphere at Anfield quietened as the crowd sensed victory was already a formality, but this didn't prevent a feeling of complacency from creeping in. Liverpool's tendency to encourage the opposition rather than extinguishing any hopes of a comeback had been a significant flaw this season. Instead of remaining ruthless and firmly shutting down any thoughts of a turnaround, Liverpool's approach allows the opposition to start believing in their chances, leading to growing momentum and, eventually, a comeback.

The warning signs were there for Liverpool as Tottenham started to gain momentum towards the end of the first half. Before their eventual goal, Tottenham had a couple of promising opportunities to score, but Liverpool failed to respond effectively to these goal-scoring chances. Eventually, Tottenham found the back of the net, capitalising on good build-up play and poor defending from Liverpool. Oliver Skipp played an excellent through-ball to Ivan Perišić, enabling Tottenham to progress into the final third. Virgil van Dijk initially tracked Perišić's run but unfortunately slipped at a crucial moment, allowing Perišić to pick out a pass into the box.

Disappointingly, Andy Robertson was the sole Liverpool defender present in the box, and his positioning needed to be better. As a result, Harry Kane found himself with an alarming amount of space and time, delivering a well-executed first-time volley that passed through Alisson's legs and found the back of the net. As a spectator, there was a concern that Tottenham might score again before halftime, which would have further swung the momentum in their favour. The goal conceded, and the shift in momentum emphasised the importance for Liverpool to regroup, reassess their approach, and make necessary adjustments to regain control of the match in the second half.

However, what unfolded in the second half can only be described as a collapse. Similar to the first goal Tottenham scored, there was a sense that another goal was imminent. Heung-min Son struck the post with a long-range effort, and

Cristian Romero came close to scoring when he stretched for a superb cross from Harry Kane, only to hit the other post.

A little later, Romero played a clever pass through to Son, who displayed excellent control and calmly slotted the ball past Alisson. Tottenham had hit the post twice in just a minute, yet Liverpool failed to heed the warning signs. The two players involved in the near misses combined to score Tottenham's second goal. It was a scenario nobody could have anticipated–Liverpool was at risk of undoing all their hard work and squandering their three-goal lead.

It had to be former Everton player Richarlison who found the equalising goal. Throughout his time on the pitch, the Anfield crowd had consistently booed him at every opportunity for his association with the blue side of Merseyside. In the build-up to the equalising goal, Tottenham was awarded a free kick following a robust tackle by James Milner on Harry Kane. Son stepped up to take the set piece, delivering a floated ball to the back post where Richarlison was waiting. He connected with the ball, which sailed over Alisson, levelling the score at 3-3. In celebration, Richarlison took off his shirt, leapt onto the advertising board in front of the Tottenham fans, gestured for silence to the Anfield crowd with a finger on his lips, and engaged in a chicken dance with

Son. It was pretty apt for Richarlison to dance in the style of a cock.

It was unforgivable to witness Liverpool surrender a three-goal lead, as it is a significant setback at any level of football. Tottenham's initial performance during the opening thirty minutes couldn't have been any worse, making them appear the inferior team that lacked motivation. However, through Liverpool's inability to maintain control and assert dominance, Tottenham managed to stage an impressive comeback and equalise the score. Despite this setback, the match still held another dramatic moment about to unfold.

In a stunning turn of events, just ninety-nine seconds after Richarlison's equalising goal, Lucas Moura committed a grave error that gifted Liverpool a late goal. While attempting to maintain possession and control the match, Moura's pass intended for his centre-back was intercepted by Diogo Jota. Seizing the golden opportunity, Jota confidently entered the box and calmly placed a beautiful finish into the far corner of the goal, restoring Liverpool's lead and making it 4-3 in the game's dying moments. This rollercoaster of a match had one final twist, leaving spectators in awe of the dramatic turn of events.

This match undoubtedly provided an exciting spectacle for neutral football fans. Even as a biased Liverpool supporter, I must admit that I still found it enjoyable despite the rollercoaster of emotions. However, I firmly believe that it is unacceptable to squander a three-goal lead. Tottenham appeared vulnerable and lacking motivation, seemingly already resigned to their fate, during the opening thirty minutes. Yet, through a combination of Liverpool easing off and Tottenham finding inspiration, they managed to mount a remarkable comeback. Liverpool must learn from this experience and ensure such a collapse doesn't happen again. Nevertheless, I am grateful that Liverpool found a way to secure all three points and put a dent in Richarlison's celebrations.

May
2023

Liverpool 1 - 0 Fulham

Premier League
Wednesday, 3rd May 2023
Anfield

Liverpool's recent run of five consecutive victories was undoubtedly a positive sign, proving Liverpool still could string together wins. Traditionally, Liverpool displays exceptional end-of-season form, often vital in intense title races or securing favourable league positions. In the 2020/21 season, their strong finish propelled them to a respectable third-place finish against challenging odds. However, their aspirations were limited this season to a fifth-place finish.

Unfortunately, Liverpool's resurgence came late in the campaign, as otherwise, there might have been a realistic chance of sneaking into the crucial fourth spot. Nevertheless, their recent form was encouraging and highlighted the team's character. In a hard-fought match against Fulham, Liverpool secured a non-aesthetically pleasing victory but ultimately delivered the desired outcome of three points. While the overall quality of the game may have been average, prioritising results is crucial, especially during these end stages of the season.

Alisson played a vital role in preserving Liverpool's lead, as he made several key saves to deny Fulham's attempts and maintain the team's advantage. The ability to grind out a win, even in these challenging circumstances, demonstrates the team's resilience and how much they have improved.

The decisive moment of the match occurred when Darwin Núñez was brought down in the box by Fulham's Issa Diop, who mistimed his clearance and made contact with Núñez instead of the ball. While the penalty decision may have been somewhat contentious upon closer inspection, Diop's clumsy challenge just about warranted the spot-kick. Taking on the responsibility, Mohamed Salah confidently struck the ball high down the middle as Bernd Leno dove to his left, successfully giving Liverpool the lead. This goal proved to be the match-winner, securing the crucial three points for Liverpool.

Darwin Núñez's performance as the leading striker for Liverpool was somewhat underwhelming. The team's recent tactical shift had yet to benefit the Uruguayan forward fully, and he sometimes appeared slightly lost on the pitch. Overall, Núñez's season has been a mixed bag. While he has performed adequately, he likely would have hoped to contribute more significantly to the team's season. With fifteen goals and four assists in all competitions, his nineteen goal-contributions can be considered acceptable for his debut season. However, as Núñez continues to settle in at Liverpool and improve his understanding of the English language, he is expected to produce even more impressive numbers in the upcoming seasons.

This led me to think about the players Liverpool bought during last year's summer transfer window. The acquisitions of Darwin Núñez, Fábio Carvalho, and Calvin Ramsay certainly raised some hindsight concerns. Unfortunately, Calvin Ramsay's time at Liverpool has been marred by injuries, significantly limiting his involvement throughout the season. He arrived at the club already carrying a back injury not initially detected during his pre-signing medical assessment.

Additionally, he suffered a knee injury during the middle of the season, further prolonging his absence from the pitch. Ramsey's injuries have prevented him from providing competition in the right-back position and rotating with Trent Alexander-Arnold as probably intended. Despite these setbacks, as a young player, Ramsay still possesses potential.

He could have a promising future at Liverpool if he can overcome his injury troubles and establish himself in the team. However, The situation was understandably disappointing, given the initial hopes for his contribution to the squad. Calvin Ramsay will be spending the 2023/24 season on loan at Preston, allowing him to get used to playing football again without the pressures of playing at a club as big as Liverpool.

Fábio Carvalho's first season at Liverpool also presented some challenges. While he is a talented player with good technical abilities, his best performances have come in the number ten attacking midfield position when playing for Fulham. However, Liverpool's style of play does not incorporate a designated number ten role, which raised questions about his fit within the team. The left-wing position is already populated with several options, such as Luis Díaz, Diogo Jota, Darwin Núñez, and even Cody Gakpo, making it difficult for Carvalho to find a place there.

Another possibility could be playing him in the left midfield position within a midfield three. Still, his performances in that role have been unimpressive, likely because it is not his natural position. The decision to sign a number ten player like Carvalho seems puzzling when

Liverpool's system does not prioritise that specific role. It is important to note that transfer decisions are often influenced by various factors, including a player's potential, versatility, and long-term development. However, it remains to be seen how Carvalho will adapt and contribute to Liverpool's setup in the future if his future is at Liverpool. There have been a few end-of-season discussions about Carvalho wanting to move away from Liverpool in search of regular football, while Liverpool prefers a loan move. It will be interesting to see what happens.

Lastly, the signing of Darwin Núñez raised questions about his role in Liverpool's system. Despite his success as a striker at Benfica, Liverpool has favoured a false-nine position rather than relying on a traditional centre-forward. This raised doubts about how Núñez fits into the team's tactical framework. The situation is reminiscent of Divock Origi's limited opportunities as an out-and-out striker in the later stages of his Liverpool career. Darwin Núñez has also been asked to play on the left wing for long periods of the season. This was likely due to injuries to Diogo Jota and Luis Díaz, but still, it felt like a makeshift way of getting Núñez game time because of his high transfer fee.

On the other hand, the addition of Cody Gakpo aligns well with Liverpool's system, as he possesses the qualities to fulfil the false-nine role effectively, especially considering Roberto Firmino's departure. However, the logic behind the other signings of Fábio Carvalho and Calvin Ramsay concerning Liverpool's system may require further explanation.

Liverpool faces a vital summer transfer window during the summer of 2023, and making shrewd signings is crucial for improving the squad. The players on the pitch, the backroom staff, and the medical department need attention. The arrival of Jörg Schmadtke, initially as a short-term director of football, is undoubtedly a step in the right direction. Even though his methods and working style are untested at a big club like Liverpool, the short-term appointment allows Liverpool to see if he is a good fit while also having someone cover a transfer window that is the most important in years.

The behind-the-scenes commotion and changes may have impacted Liverpool's performance this season. It's natural to have problems with disruptions or transitions within the backroom structure. The club must address these issues, stabilise the backroom operations, and ensure an efficient setup in the future. There is absolutely no more room for complacency.

Liverpool 1 - 0 Brentford

Premier League
Saturday, 6th May 2023
Anfield

Winning had become ingrained in Liverpool's recent form, extending their winning streak to six matches and maintaining an unbeaten run of eight games. Although Liverpool was just one point behind fourth-placed Manchester United, Liverpool had played two more matches, making securing a top-four finish increasingly challenging. The missed opportunities and dropped points throughout the season seemed likely to cost Liverpool a place in the top four.

An intriguing statistic emerged after the match, revealing that the time the ball was in play during the game amounted to a mere forty-three minutes and ten seconds, accounting for just 44% of the total match duration. This figure represents the lowest recorded playtime for any Liverpool game in the Premier League since records began in 2006. It highlighted the significant time the game was paused, whether due to stoppages, fouls, or other factors, resulting in limited actual gameplay.

Liverpool displayed a notable change in their approach, showing a resolute determination and refusing to be intimidated or dominated by their opponents. The team showed a heightened level of aggression, which was particularly refreshing considering their relatively passive performances earlier in the season. Liverpool anticipated a physical encounter against Brentford and responded in kind with their assertive style of play. This display of resilience and refusal to be bullied was enjoyable to watch. It's commendable that Liverpool demonstrated their willingness to stand up to teams that attempt to increase their aggression levels when facing them, proving that the players are more than capable of rising to the challenge. If only we had seen this mentality earlier in the season.

Liverpool's opening goal was a result of a well-executed team effort. Fabinho cleverly lofted a pass towards the back post, precisely aimed for Virgil van Dijk, who had ventured forward for a corner kick. Virgil displayed his aerial prowess by nodding the ball back across the goalmouth. Mohamed Salah showed his goal-scoring instincts, forcing the ball into the net with his second touch after miss-hitting his first attempt. This goal held special significance as it marked another record broken by Salah.

Mohamed Salah's remarkable achievement of scoring in nine consecutive matches at Anfield solidified his place in Liverpool's history books. Considering the illustrious players who have graced the club throughout its history, it is an extraordinary feat. None of them were able to achieve such a remarkable record. Salah's goal-scoring prowess was on full display this season, with an impressive tally of thirty goals in all competitions, accompanied by sixteen assists. This marks the fourth time Salah surpassed the thirty-goal mark in the last six seasons. After the match, Salah spoke about breaking another record and how happy he is at Liverpool:

It means a lot to me, like I've said before, I feel at home here. I'm happy, and hopefully, we just need to finish the season in the best possible way. But as much as I'm scoring goals, the team winning is the most important thing.

In the first half, there was a golden opportunity for Darwin Núñez to score when Trent Alexander-Arnold delivered a perfectly placed pass from the defensive-midfield position, bypassing the Brentford defence and sending Núñez through on goal in a one-on-one situation with the goalkeeper. It was the kind of chance Núñez would have easily converted during his time at Benfica. However, due to his lack of confidence and game time, he failed to make contact with the ball and ultimately missed the opportunity to score. Seeing him not capitalising on such a clear-cut chance wasn't very pleasant. Darwin Núñez is a player who heavily relies on confidence, and it appeared that he was overthinking and struggling to find his rhythm.

Bryan Mbeumo celebrated as he found the back of the net for Brentford, but his goal was rightfully disallowed for offside. Fortunately for Liverpool, Brentford struggled to create significant chances that tested their defence. At the other end, Cody Gakpo had a couple of opportunities to score and secure Liverpool's second goal. However, he was unable to convert either chance.

One notable instance saw Diogo Jota deliver a powerful cross across the goalmouth, and Gakpo was unfortunate as the ball hit him but failed to find the back of the net. Another opportunity came from a defensive mistake by Brentford's Aaron Hickey. Under pressure from Salah, Hickey accidentally headed the ball into his box. Gakpo controlled the loose ball with his chest and volleyed wide of the near post. Gakpo's visible disappointment highlighted his frustration at missing a gifted opportunity on goal.

It was understandable and wise to approach the remaining matches cautiously to keep hopes from getting too high after experiencing disappointments and false dawns earlier in the season. However, this weekend's results certainly worked in Liverpool's favour, but maintaining a realistic expectation of finishing in the Europa League spots was wise. While Liverpool still had a slim chance to secure fourth place, it was essential to balance optimism and practicality to avoid the eventual heartbreak of finishing fifth.

Leicester City 0 - 3 Liverpool

Premier League
Monday, 15th May 2023
King Power Stadium

Liverpool had one job, and that was to win at whatever cost. Playing on Monday night, Liverpool knew every other result from the weekend's football. Although Manchester United had won with a 2-0 home victory against Wolverhampton, Newcastle had dropped two points with a draw at Elland Road against Leeds. A win for Liverpool against relegation-threatened Leicester City would move Liverpool one point behind Newcastle and Manchester United, albeit having played a game more.

Interestingly, Newcastle striker Callum Wilson had been talking about Newcastle and their top-four hopes. Speaking on the BBC's Footballer's Football Podcast, Wilson joked:

Liverpool needs to relax! I said I could smell [a top-four finish] a couple of weeks ago. Now that scent is gone. I don't know where it's gone. I can't find it!

Pressure can make teams do crazy things, so I hoped that if Wilson was feeling the pressure from Liverpool's late top-four charge, his teammates and Newcastle's management were feeling it too. Liverpool needed to keep the pressure on Newcastle with a win against Leicester, a team running out of chances to accumulate enough points to survive relegation. On a Monday night, the King Power would always be tricky, but the Reds were comfortable and secured an impressive 3-0 victory.

There had been much focus on Trent Alexander-Arnold following his transition to the inverted fullback role. However, it is essential to acknowledge the contributions of Curtis Jones, the other local talent in our team. Curtis had shown remarkable growth and maturity in his performances, displaying his technical skills, versatility, and a strong understanding of Liverpool's tactics. His development was considered positive this late in the season, and it was essential to appreciate his contributions in these matches.

Seeing Curtis Jones thriving and proving his worth in the Liverpool team was a welcome sight. Sometimes, it takes a consistent run of games and a boost in confidence for a player to showcase their abilities. Jones' recent performances, including his standout display against Leicester City, demonstrated his quality and potential. It's understandable to have doubts or reservations about him, but his form and impact on the team changed perceptions. Jones's ability to maintain his performance over a consecutive run of games was a testament to his growth and development as a player. Witnessing his progress and anticipating his continued contributions to the Liverpool squad is exciting.

Jones' opening goal showed his composure and technique in front of the goal. The sequence of play leading up to the goal involved some excellent team coordination and execution. From Alisson's long ball up the pitch, Luis Díaz won a header he directed backwards, and Jordan Henderson collected the ball. Henderson played the ball out wide to Mohamed Salah, who delivered a pinpoint cross that found Jones at the back post. Jones displayed excellent control and precision to guide the ball into the net with finesse, highlighting his calmness, as it would have been easy to overhit the shot and miss the golden chance.

Jones' second goal showed his sharpness in the penalty area and the positive impact of his newfound confidence. The build-up play leading to the goal showed Cody Gakpo's skill in turning and driving at the defence, while Salah's quick and precise pass set up Jones for the finish. With the confidence gained from his earlier goal, Jones displayed composure as he controlled the ball with his right foot, turned, and executed a well-placed half-volley into the far side of the net.

The match continued to be under Liverpool's control in the second half, with Leicester finding it difficult to pose a significant threat. While Alisson had to make a crucial save to preserve the clean sheet, Liverpool's defensive solidity kept the opposition at bay. The comfortable lead allowed the away fans to show their appreciation as they serenaded Roberto Firmino, recognising his contributions to the team before he departed in the summer. The singing was briefly interrupted when Trent Alexander-Arnold added a third goal to solidify Liverpool's dominance further.

Liverpool was awarded a valuable free-kick opportunity right on the edge of Leicester City's penalty area. Mohamed Salah positioned himself to take the kick and rolled it back a few yards, effectively registering his third assist of the game. In seizing the opportunity, Trent Alexander-Arnold swiftly approached the ball and unleashed a powerful and accurate shot into the top right corner of the net. Overjoyed with his successful strike, Trent rushed towards the corner flag, where he celebrated by sliding on his knees and offering a nonchalant shrug. This gesture has become his signature celebration.

After the final whistle, a heartwarming moment unfolded as the Liverpool players approached the away end to express their gratitude to the travelling supporters. The chants dedicated to Roberto Firmino persisted, creating an atmosphere of affection and appreciation. The players, displaying camaraderie, gathered around Firmino, urging him to revel in the adulation. Playfully, they nudged him towards the away fans, wholeheartedly joining in the celebration by enthusiastically leaping and rejoicing alongside him. The beautiful scene exemplified the strong bond between the players and the passionate supporters.

It was unfortunate that Liverpool's strong form at the business end of the season was not enough to secure a top-four position. The outcome of the season now relied on factors beyond their control. For Liverpool to have a chance of finishing in the top four, either Manchester United *or* Newcastle would need to stumble in multiple matches, with Liverpool having to win their remaining fixtures. Given the limited number of games that remained and the requirement for specific results, it proved too much of a challenge for Liverpool.

Liverpool 1 - 1 Aston Villa

Premier League
Saturday, 20th May 2023
Anfield

The season's conclusion may not have unfolded as we had hoped. Still, Roberto Firmino's eighty-ninth-minute equaliser provided a touch of magic, and the closest Liverpool came to a fairytale ending. The match proved quite frustrating for Liverpool, with the referee appearing reluctant to award decisions in favour of the home team and Aston Villa showcasing an almost flawless defensive performance that proved difficult to break down. Nevertheless, salvaging a draw allowed Liverpool to avoid the disappointment of concluding the campaign with a home defeat on a day that held significant farewells.

Aston Villa rightfully earned a penalty in the twenty-second minute of the match. Ibrahima Konaté lunged to win the ball from Ollie Watkins, who had timed his run to perfection to get on the end of a lovely pass from John McGinn. The partnership between Watkins and McGinn caused trouble for Liverpool multiple times during the match.

Konaté received a caution with a yellow card, and Watkins took the penalty in front of the Kop end. Luckily for Liverpool, Watkins missed the target, shooting the ball just past the post. It was a fortunate escape for Liverpool.

A recurring pattern this season has been Liverpool's failure to recognise the warning signs, even when they are glaringly obvious. Five minutes after the missed penalty, Aston Villa scored a well-executed goal. Douglas Luiz delivered a precise pass from a central position to the back post, where Jacob Ramsey displayed composure to sidefoot the ball past Alisson calmly. It was an impressive goal that handed Villa the lead. However, Ramsey's celebration, where he held a finger up to his ear while running towards the corner of the Kop, felt unnecessary.

I have never been a fan of Tyrone Mings, and one of the reasons might seem trivial, but it bothers me nonetheless. It's his constant chewing of gum, which gives off an air of nonchalance. Perhaps he does it to project a sense of calm and composure, but personally, it irritates me. There was a significant incident during the match where Mings should have been shown a red card, which only grew in significance when he went on to win the Player-of-the-Match award.

During the first half, Tyrone Mings went in for a challenge, leading with his foot, and caught Cody Gakpo in the abdomen. It appeared that Mings used a significant amount of force, and considering that Gakpo would have had a clear opportunity on goal if not for Mings' dangerous tackle, the decision only to show a yellow card seemed baffling.

To make matters more bewildering, VAR reviewed the incident but didn't prompt referee John Brooks to review it on the pitchside screen. This suggested that VAR agreed with the initial decision of a yellow card. I have viewed it multiple times and seen the picture circulated on social media of the visible stud marks left on Cody Gakpo's abdomen and chest due to Mings' boot. Why was it not deemed a red card offence? Unsurprisingly, this wasn't the only instance of controversial refereeing during the match.

After the game, a fan suggested that Liverpool is still paying the "Tierney tax." It implied that referees intentionally denied Liverpool any favourable decisions due to the altercation between Jürgen Klopp and Paul Tierney a few weeks earlier. This incident resulted in Klopp being suspended, forcing him to watch this match from the stands and communicate with the dugout via an earpiece. I usually try to remove bias, so I don't look at everything Liverpool-related with rose-tinted glasses. Still, it's hard to ignore the questionable refereeing we witnessed recently.

The entire second half was frustrating for Liverpool. Aston Villa used time-wasting tactics whenever possible, which often went unpunished by the officials. Coupled with their effective low-block tactics, this made it increasingly difficult for Liverpool to break through. Cody Gakpo thought he had found the back of the net, but the referees had other ideas.

Trent Alexander-Arnold delivered a deep ball to the back post, similar to Douglas Luiz's earlier assist. Luis Díaz headed the ball backwards, hoping to set up a better opportunity for a player in a better shooting position. Unfortunately, Díaz's header inadvertently struck Villa defender Ezri Konsa, and the ball landed at the feet of Virgil van Dijk, who was in an offside position. Without delving too deeply into the rest of the play, Gakpo eventually scored, but VAR intervened. The goal was reviewed by referee John Brooks, who viewed the incident on the pitchside screen and swiftly disallowed it for offside. The frustration was building.

As the clock ticked closer to the final whistle, Roberto Firmino, Liverpool's Brazillian number nine, delivered one more moment of jubilation at Anfield with an equalising goal. This goal would mark his last-ever professional goal at

Anfield. The goal came from a superb delivery from Mohamed Salah, who played a precise ball from the right side of the box using the outside of his left foot. Firmino showed determination as he launched himself off the ground, fully committing to making contact with the ball and ensuring it went into the net. It demonstrated his unwavering commitment one final time.

Sadly, Liverpool couldn't find a winning goal, and the match ended in a draw, ending Liverpool's seven-match winning streak. The match's outcome quickly faded into the background as the club started the leaving ceremony for the players set to leave Liverpool in the summer. The entire squad and staff formed a guard of honour, paying tribute to the contributions of Roberto Firmino, James Milner, Alex Oxlade-Chamberlain, and Naby Keïta. Each player was given a memento from the CEO Billy Hogan and Liverpool legend Sir Kenny Dalglish.

Following the ceremony, an intriguing revelation surfaced during an on-field interview with LFC TV. James Milner appeared to disclose some unknown information about him leaving the club. Milner said that the club went against the wishes of manager jürgen Klopp by declining his request for Milner to get a contract extension. This was unexpected and intriguing as Klopp's wants have typically been accommodated in the past. After Liverpool's average season, I wonder if club officials have decided to be more active in decisions involving the club to avoid repeating what happened this season. It is only speculation on my part, but it feels like something might have changed.

Southampton 4 - 4 Liverpool

Premier League
Sunday, 28th May 2023
Saint Mary's Stadium

In a match lacking any significance in terms of league standings, both Liverpool and Southampton found themselves in a dead-rubber situation. With Liverpool having secured fifth place and Southampton already relegated, the game outcome was unimportant for either team. However, it is always disheartening to witness Liverpool's struggles, even in a match that ultimately has no impact on the final standings. It serves as a reminder of the high standards and expectations surrounding the club, regardless of the circumstances.

Jürgen Klopp's decision to change the team lineup was understandable, considering the lack of importance. The inclusion of Caoimhín Kelleher in the goal, the absence of Virgil van Dijk, and the decision to give James Milner and Roberto Firmino a farewell start reflected a sense of rotation and a gesture of farewell. The season-ending provided an opportunity to give playing time to different players and pay tribute to those who have made significant contributions to the club.

Arthur Melo, the loan signing who did not feature in *any* Premier League match this season, was on the bench and did not feature. It raised an important point about the value and impact of signings. While financial considerations are crucial, assessing a player's overall contribution to the team is equally vital. This situation serves as a reminder that prioritising the cheapest option may not be the best option. This is an essential lesson for the club's owners, FSG, when making future transfer decisions.

The match began with Liverpool swiftly taking a two-goal lead. The first goal came courtesy of a gift from Southampton. As the south coast club attempted to play the ball out from the back, Roméo Lavia received the ball in his penalty area and played a blind pass for centre-back Jan Bednarek. Diogo Jota, displaying quick thinking, intercepted the pass and seized the opportunity to slot the ball into the relatively empty net. From a Southampton perspective, it was an unfortunate and avoidable goal, but Liverpool took the gift and found themselves in the lead.

Moments later, Roberto Firmino added to Liverpool's lead, scoring his thirteenth goal of the season and bidding farewell to the club in style. Once again, Trent Alexander-Arnold played a perfectly executed line-splitting pass, finding Firmino's compatriot Fabinho at the edge of the Southampton box. Fabinho passed the ball to Firmino, who showed his agility by skillfully dribbling into the penalty area, deceiving both Southampton centre-backs with a feigned shot. Exploiting the opening, Firmino took another touch towards the goal before calmly slotting the ball through the legs of goalkeeper Alex McCarthy. It was a poignant moment, witnessing Firmino's last goal. His contributions to the team will be sorely missed. Adiós, señor.

Despite Liverpool's dominant start, the match took an unexpected turn as Southampton began to find their rhythm and capitalised on the opportunities presented to them. With the home crowd behind them, Southampton gained confidence and started to mount a comeback, sensing an opportunity to salvage some pride from their final game of the season. Liverpool's complacency allowed Southampton back into the contest, injecting a sense of drama into what initially seemed like a foregone conclusion.

James Ward-Prowse scored the first goal to spark Southampton's comeback. Carlos Alcaraz, positioned on the right wing, showed exceptional skill as he manoeuvred through a crowd of Liverpool players, advancing towards the box. Alcaraz then executed a precise one-two pass with Kamaldeen Sulemana, who returned the ball to him. With good technique, Alcaraz played an outside-of-the-boot pass to find Ward-Prowse, who struck a well-placed, curling shot past Kelleher and into the back of the net. The goal injected renewed hope and momentum into the Southampton team, signalling the beginning of their comeback.

For Southampton's second goal, Roberto Firmino was dispossessed in midfield by a well-timed tackle from Roméo Lavia. The ball fell to the feet of Theo Walcott, who quickly took the opportunity and played a through ball to Kamaldeen Sulemana. With calm composure, Sulemana struck the ball first time, beyond Kelleher's reach, to find the back of the net to score his first goal for Southampton. Liverpool's defensive lapse had led to another setback, and little did they know that further challenges awaited them.

In the second half, Sulemana, undoubtedly full of confidence from his previous goal, made a remarkable solo run from deep within Southampton's half. He showed his dribbling skills by dribbling past Fabinho with ease, and the defence hesitated to close him down, meaning Sulemana was fast approaching the edge of Liverpool's penalty area.

Sulemana unleashed a well-placed shot that nestled into the corner of the goal, granting Southampton the lead in the match. While the outcome held little significance in the larger context, it was undoubtedly frustrating to witness Fabinho's lackadaisical approach, allowing Sulemana to glide past him so effortlessly. This issue had happened far too often this season, and I wouldn't be against signing another defensive midfielder in the summer transfer window to add some steel back to Liverpool's midfield.

In an unfortunate turn of events for Liverpool, Southampton not only staged an impressive comeback from being two goals down, but they also extended their lead by adding another goal. Shortly after his introduction as a substitute, Jordan Henderson received the ball in midfield but made a costly error with his pass, gifting it directly to Adam Armstrong. Grabbing the opportunity, Armstrong dribbled towards the Liverpool goal before unleashing a low shot that beat Kelleher. Recognising his mistake, Henderson apologised, acknowledging the consequences of his poor pass that resulted in Liverpool conceding another goal.

I don't want to be overly critical of Kelleher, especially being dropped into the team cold with a heavily rotated defence in front of him, but he could have done better with some of the goals conceded. It is challenging because we are so used to seeing Alisson in goal, so it isn't fair to compare Kelleher with one of the best goalkeepers in the world. On a personal note, Kelleher probably felt he could have done better with some of the goals.

It was a rollercoaster of a match for Liverpool. Despite surrendering their lead and trailing by two goals against a team already relegated, they showed determination to mount a comeback. It would have been straightforward for Liverpool to give up, waiting for the final whistle to end the match and the season, but scoring two goals to level the score at 4-4 was commendable, at least.

Liverpool's third goal resulted from a well-coordinated and fluid team effort. Starting from Diogo Jota on the right wing, he delivered a precise pass towards the centre to find Harvey Elliott positioned just outside the penalty area. With a deft touch, Elliott quickly redirected the ball to Trent, who had made an intelligent run on the right side of the penalty area. Trent took full advantage of the opportunity and sent a low and powerful cross across the box. Cody Gakpo displayed great anticipation and positioning as he calmly tapped the ball into the net to complete the well-executed goal. The sequence of passes and the timing of the movements showed Liverpool's quality in attack.

For Liverpool's equalising goal, Mohamed Salah, positioned centrally, showed precision by playing a perfectly weighted through ball to Diogo Jota. Jota unleashed a powerful first-time shot towards the near post, leaving Southampton goalkeeper Alex McCarthy with little chance to make a save. The goal completed Liverpool's comeback, levelling the score at 4-4. While the match was a rollercoaster of emotions, it served as a reminder of the areas that Liverpool still needs to address in the transfer window. Despite maintaining their unbeaten run of eleven games, the performance highlighted the need for reinforcements.

The final whistle echoed at St. Mary's Stadium, marking the match's conclusion and season-ending. Finishing fifth place and securing a spot in the Europa League for the 2023/24 season evoked mixed emotions among supporters. While the Europa League presents an opportunity for Liverpool to compete in a European tournament, it falls short of the prestigious Champions League, leaving a sense of unfulfillment.

Looking ahead, Liverpool fans remain hopeful for the future. The prospect of improving the squad with new signings brings anticipation and the desire to reclaim their position among the top teams in the game. The aim is to regroup, strengthen the team, and once again challenge at the highest level. With the right additions, Liverpool's aspirations to return to the pinnacle of football could be within reach.

Final Thoughts On The Season

I was initially going to title this book 'Transition'. It was a keyword that featured everywhere during the season's early stages to explain Liverpool's poor performances and form. "Liverpool is in a transition season" was a way of saying they aren't doing well, and it felt like an excuse. I am still figuring out what Liverpool was transitioning to or from, other than transitioning from a team that used to win almost every week to one that didn't.

I finally settled on the title 'Losing Intensity' after reading Pepijn Lijnders' book, 'Intensity'. Pep's book was full of positive words and praise for the team's mentality and work ethic. They were the mentality monsters, after all. However, reading quotes like 'Intensity is our identity while witnessing Liverpool's continued lack of it was frustrating, and the irony wasn't lost on me.

The tricky thing was that Liverpool supporters hoped that Liverpool would compete for the Premier League title this season. However, as the season progressed, it became clear that the team faced numerous challenges and setbacks. It is not uncommon for fans to have optimistic expectations for their beloved club, driven by their passion and loyalty. Nevertheless, it was necessary to reassess and adjust our aims based on the realities and circumstances that unfolded throughout the season.

The season had its ups and downs, with memorable and forgettable moments. The team experienced victories and defeats against varying levels of opponents, showcasing their strengths and vulnerabilities. While impressive scorelines against teams like Bournemouth, Manchester United and Rangers brought joy to the fans, the losses to Real Madrid, Leeds, Bournemouth, and Nottingham Forest, to name a few, left a bitter taste. The ultimate assessment of the season will be influenced by the failure to secure a top-four finish and qualify for the Champions League. Something that wasn't even fathomable at the start of the campaign.

A season in the Europa League beckons, and supporters should maintain a balanced perspective to avoid underestimating the challenges in the competition next season. While the desire to reach the final and emerge victorious is natural, Liverpool will encounter tough competition from teams eager to defeat them and claim the prestigious "We beat Liverpool" badge. Early predictions of Liverpool reaching the final in Dublin, Ireland, should be met with caution to avoid setting ourselves up for more disappointment. I know fans who have already booked the trip to the final, I wish I had that optimism, and I hope their efforts to book it early weren't in vain. Still, football is based on hope and ambition, so who am I to dampen spirits? I don't want another season of disappointment and misery.

The excuses of injuries and a depleted squad because of the previous season's quadruple chase got very dull quickly. Don't get me wrong, some of the players were fatigued, and rightly so. The squad had played every match available the season before, with the shortest summer break before having to do it all again. *Supporters* were exhausted, so I can't imagine how the players must have felt.

Nonetheless, Liverpool got their pre-season all wrong in the lead-up to the season, and Jürgen Klopp even accepted that the tour to Asia disrupted their schedule. They are going to Asia again in the summer of 2023. Let's hope they have learnt their lesson and won't repeat the wrongdoings. Pre-season is to help improve the player's fitness and team tactics, not sap their energy before a gruelling season.

FSG's self-sufficient business model at Liverpool means that the club operates within its financial means, primarily relying on revenue generated from sponsorships, gate receipts, television rights, and player sales. Liverpool's approach to player acquisitions will be closely watched as the summer transfer window approaches. The club has been patient, waiting for the right player rather than making hasty signings. While there were speculations about Jude Bellingham being a target, recent reports suggest that Liverpool pulled out of the race to avoid a bidding war. Real Madrid confirmed the signing of Bellingham shortly after the season ended.

Liverpool's midfield is an area that requires significant attention and investment for a rebuild. However, Liverpool's traditional approach of not spending without selling a player first, like selling Philippe Coutinho to Barcelona, was an example of how Liverpool has balanced the books before making significant financial investments in incoming players. It remains to be seen how Liverpool will navigate the upcoming transfer window and address their midfield needs while adhering to their self-sustaining financial model. The option of FSG seeking external investment has gone quiet, meaning the owners have unlikely secured financial investment for transfers. The jury will be out if FSG fails to deliver.

Despite the challenges and setbacks faced this season, there remains a sense of cautious optimism among Liverpool supporters. The presence of Jürgen Klopp as the manager is a source of confidence, given his track record of improving teams through shrewd signings and tactical adjustments. However, there is a recognition that there can be no more room for complacency or errors moving forward.

If this season has taught me anything, it is not to take winning for granted. When Liverpool is in winning form and getting positive results weekly, it is effortless to overlook the work that goes into the player's performances and concentrate on the three points. It has also shown me how erratic football is and how we, as fans, go through those highs and lows in only a few days, from the jubilant joys of scoring seven past United to losing to Bournemouth six days later. I need to learn how to navigate these emotions better so my mood and well-being aren't affected by outcomes out of my control. It is challenging, but writing this book has helped.

To return to their best, Liverpool must approach the upcoming season with renewed determination and dedication. The players must be willing to give their all and go the extra mile for the manager and the team. With the right mindset, hard work, and a few strategic signings to strengthen the squad, Liverpool can potentially compete for trophies in the 2023/24 season. The hope is that the team can rediscover their winning form and bring more silverware to Anfield.

Acknowledgements

I adore Liverpool Football Club, and during the COVID-19 lockdowns, I became a bookworm, enjoying reading and writing more than ever. This is why I embarked on the ambitious journey of writing this book, combining two hobbies I enjoy. The book was filled with triumphs and challenges; creating it has been a deeply personal and fulfilling experience. I hope you enjoyed reading it, considering the effort that went into its creation.

It has also been a cathartic experience, allowing me to navigate the rollercoaster of emotions that accompanied what can only be described as a rather average season for Liverpool. It provided an outlet to express the highs and lows, the frustrations and moments of joy that defined the team's season. Through my writing, I aimed to capture the feelings of those experiences and share them with fellow fans who have undoubtedly felt the same emotions.

May this book reflect our collective journey and offer solace, understanding, comfort, and unity among supporters who have stood by Liverpool through thick and thin.

Thank you for purchasing this book. I appreciate the support and hope you enjoyed it despite 2022/23 not being a memorable season. Like you, I eagerly await Jürgen Klopp's Liverpool 2.0, and I am confident it is just around the corner.

YNWA

Printed in Great Britain
by Amazon

31193839R00209